CALVIN MILLER

author of The Singer

A HUNGER FOR
MEANING

INTER-VARSITY PRESS
DOWNERS GROVE
ILLINOIS 60515

Library of Congress Cataloging in Publication Data

Miller, Calvin.
    A hunger for meaning.

    Includes bibliographical references.
    1. Apologetics—20th century. I. Title.
BT1102.M535   1984   239   83-26490
ISBN 0-87784-830-0

20   19   18   17   16   15   14   13   12   11   10   9   8   7   6   5   4   3   2   1
99   98   97   96   95   94   93   92   91   90   89   88   87   86   85   84

So I go on, not knowing,
—I would not, if I might—
I would rather walk in the dark with God
Than go alone in the light.
Mary Gardner Brainard

Most of the time the fact that this fact is impossible doesn't
bother me. I live by the impossible. Like the White Queen, I
find it a good discipline to practice believing as many as
seven impossible things every morning before breakfast.
Madeleine L'Engle

Doubt my sanity but acknowledge my immortality.
William Lloyd Garrison

I
Reason and Faith: Quarrelsome Brothers

REASON IS A CYNIC. Fanged and ravenous, it circles faith, grinning in triumph, demanding something illogical to feed on. Reason often views belief as inflamed emotionalism void of thought.

Cynicism is usually the aggressor in the war with faith. Militant thinkers from great universities often pose questions that throw believers into shock. In the numbing silence that follows, the arts and sciences sail on through sizeable, important arguments. Looking over the great Christian creeds, reason asks with belittling arrogance, "Is that all?"

Faith, on the other hand, is an optimist. Kind and hopeful, it stands in the icy gales of doubt, seldom dressed for the severe weather it has to endure. Faith is no quitter. It confronts logic boldly but it moves slowly. Scorned by doubt, it smiles and inches its way forward. It welcomes antagonists to the warm fires of meaning that it lights in any arctic of academic thought.

Quarrelsome Twins

Reason and faith, however, are close relatives, perhaps brothers. These brothers both seek meaning but they are quarrelsome twins who from the womb claw at each other's dignity. They often compete for disciples, offering different rewards to those who choose to follow. Reason offers his followers airtight arguments and the last word in every conversation. Faith offers warm mystery and inner meaning to those who are disenchanted with cold, hard mechanical facts.

In the last quarter of the twentieth century, however, believers have become more studious and bold. At long last, they are hurling back some questions of their own. Creationists have demanded that scientists quit offering theory as law. Pro-life activists are asking for sensible definitions of the beginning of life. Christian thinkers are stiffening their spines and lifting their chins and stating clearly their right to be involved in the serious issues of our day. Believers are thinkers. Serious believers are serious thinkers. Faith and thought do not cancel each other out.

Still, believers are not welcomed into the world of ideas by secular thinkers. The old dread emerges and confronts us as Christians. We are still considered second-class scholars. Our minds are not to be trusted. Articles, movies, books and the theater reinforce this stereotype. Intelligent men of faith are hounded by the unsettled feeling that religious truth is antiquated and beside the point.

To follow Christ is to defend his church. So we remind ourselves that "the powers of death shall not prevail against it" (Mt 16:18). Confidently, we recall the words of the psalmist that "the fool says in his heart, 'There is no God'" (Ps 14:1; 53:1). We defend, but we are apprehensive in the presence of the philosophers. We cower before their arrogance and we feel unprepared to reply.

Faith is the substance and meaning of life but believers are hard-pressed to convince those who disbelieve. Cynics do not want to know what we believe. They think they know *what*. They want to know *why*. *Why* is a question of anguish. Out of anguish believers want to answer the hard issues of doubt. They want to satisfy the skeptics. Yet they seldom do. For God will not stand still. He is near but invisible. He is evident but retiring. His reality seems to roar around us, but only in overpowering silence. Our small logic cannot contain his vastness. And there are even times when our reaching spirits cannot touch him. Sometimes he seems to listen. Sometimes he is elsewhere. When God retreats, belief, however ardent, is brother to doubt. But just as believers may doubt, unbelievers from time to time are hungry, reaching for something real to fill the emptiness of their lives. Such skeptics, in times of honesty, confess that their hypotheses are no answer to their deepest longings. Unexpectedly they find themselves inching toward faith.

Belief and doubt are thus not rigid categories. Believers doubt from time to time, and doubters sometimes believe. We who are men and women of faith seek like cynics, but we do it with two sets of eyes. With outer eyes we hope to discover new scientific reality. But our great discoveries are made with inner eyes. The object of our inner search finds a glorious reality. God is there. So is his kingdom.

Atheists, those calculating, professional doubters, see no inconsistency in living in the middle of an all-pervading God and looking past him. They shake their fists at God, daring him to be. Standing in the very middle of God they doubt him; it is as if they stood in the Grand Canyon and denied the Colorado River. The cosmoswide God, unacknowledged by the cynics, is still the vast arena where all human struggle takes place. It is impossible for any atheist to step outside of God and deny his being. He must deny God from the very heart of the Almighty.

There are no imaginary boundaries that say, "God begins here." *"In him we live and move and have our being"!* (Acts 17:28). To discover God is merely to open our eyes. People sometimes ask, "How did you find God?" I often say, "I found God pretty much like a fish discovers water. I opened my eyes and gills and heart. There was such a rush of God into my life that it would have been impossible not to discover him."

Zealots and Zombies

I want to accomplish three things in this book. First of all, I would like to challenge Christians to a bold new level of contemporary Christian thinking. We cannot defend what we do not understand. Christians immersed in a technological world know more about logic and science than they do the Bible. They seem lost in the gap between a bright technology and spiritual reality.

The challenge of the apostle Paul to Timothy was "Study to shew thyself approved" (2 Tim 2:15 KJV). Perhaps Paul's admonition to modern believers would be, "Study to survive!" It is naive to feel that intellectual matters are irrelevant in the pursuit of Christ. This is a day of intense education. Contented ignorance leaves us cut off from the world of thought and commerce we are called by Christ to redeem.

Christianity has too often had a merely emotional approach to worship. In the wake of neo-Pentecostalism, we have been prone to step up our emotions while gearing down our intellects. Revivalism can produce Christians infatuated with feeling their faith rather than knowing it. New converts often become satisfied with a gelatinous "chummy-ism" that shakes with fervor but is without substance. This naiveté leaves us powerless to answer the skeptics. Ours are desperate times.

But in our tangled age most of us are largely truants whose disinterest in theology and culture is unthinkable.

William James once said that to most people religion was either an acute fever or a dull habit. He seems to have described both his day and ours. Fevers are unhealthy—let all zealots be reminded! Habits are mindless and reflexive—let all zombies take note! In contented ignorance, we replace our service to God with religious routines. Even if our dull habits have all the elements of joy, no faith can change the world that does not change people. I'm reminded of the cliché once spoken of people leaving church: "They're praising God on Sunday; they'll be all right on Monday. It's just a little habit they've acquired."

A second goal of this book is to help seekers find an intelligent confidence in Christianity. I want them to be able to do more than agree to certain truths. My hope is that they will be able to give their wholehearted acceptance. Faith can only be sure when the mind endorses all that the heart embraces.

We who believe also need to remember that in Christ there is hope for all—even hard-core cynics. For their hope lies in our willingness to talk to them. Thus we must rid ourselves of the fear of dialog.

Seeking skeptics have a hunger for meaning and might be induced to eat at a table where the fare is made nutritious by Christians who study. If we studied and talked and listened, doubters might rise from our cerebral meal to tell others that there *is* something solid in the Christian broth after all. Thus we may make disciples and find our own hunger for meaning satisfied at the same time.

Study gives surety in the showdown. I cannot imagine the apostle Paul being unsure of himself in his critical defense before Nero. Knowing that the gospel of Christ "is the power of God for salvation" (Rom 1:16) enabled Paul to stand alone before the emperor. "At my first defense no one took my part; all deserted me. May it not be charged against them! But the Lord stood by me and gave me strength to proclaim the message fully, that all the Gentiles might hear it. So I was rescued from the lion's mouth" (2 Tim 4:16-17). Paul was almost certainly martyred after this final stand. But his martyrdom is not as important as his magnificent confidence that in an empty universe something was worth dying for.

Martyrdom points to an essential aspect of faith. Great ideas are more important than the person who presents them. The proclamation actually endorses the proclaimer. When I hear the word *Marx* I do not immediately think of his picture. I think of his ideas—class struggle, socialism, communism and so on. Only gradually do the faint outlines of his physical image emerge. I then recall that he was bearded, high of brow, with deep and wide-set, piercing eyes. But I hear his cause before I see his face.

The same is true for Paul of Tarsus. He is not primarily a physical image. If we think a moment we can recall the impressions of the painters and novelists—his shortened frame, his rounded shoulders, his bald pate. But before we see his image, his message emerges. "When I came to you, brethren, I did not come proclaiming to you the testimony of God in lofty words or wisdom. For I decided to know nothing among you except Jesus Christ and him crucified" (1 Cor 2:1-2).

Paul's studied certainty had driven out the witches of doubt. He never said, "For to me to live is Christ, *I think*," or, "God was *probably* in Christ reconciling the world unto himself." His was a certain trumpet: "I know whom I have believed" (2 Tim 1:12).

Ideas live for centuries after those who first declared them are gone. It is fascinating to watch a cynic clawing at the arguments of a man long dead. The dead thinker does not slow the vital thought he left behind. In fury, his argument slashes at living adversaries. Paul is not a dead argument, only a dead man. The philosopher Bertrand Russell, with all of his brilliance, twenty centuries after the fact still debated him. Russell's disagreement with Paul prompted the popular publication *Why I Am Not a Christian* which sternly set agnosticism against grace twenty centuries later.

Creed-Dwellers

I have one final goal in this book. I want to challenge Christians not only to believe but to demonstrate their faith. No creed is merely devotional. Creeds create lifestyles. They spawn strong reasons to live and bold arguments of grace. Belief must act and argue or it will not endure.

Marx once again serves to illustrate. Suppose Communists met one day a week and read *The Communist Manifesto,* sang songs about it, and heard a speech on it. Then suppose they went out to live like Republicans or Tsarists or Capitalists. Communists are a world threat because they are "creed-dwellers."

It is easier by far to argue with creedal thinking than it is to argue with creedal living. Consider what inconsistent living has done to build hypocrisy into the Apostles' Creed. "I believe in God the Father Almighty . . ." but see myself as sovereign and self-directed. When believing becomes incidental to doing, faith lies down beside a ready grave.

No wonder the poet has rhymed our "thumb-worn creeds" with our "large professions and our little deeds." And remember James's admonition: "Be doers of the word [the creed] and not hearers only, deceiving yourselves" (Jas 1:22). Living a belief is substance. Thinking one is vacuous.

Christians must hold to faith while their hands are full. In the press of too much talking we must recite the creeds. Doing reinforces what is taught: acting out a creed makes the learning of it sure. When Paul first met Christ, he was uncertain, crying out, "Who are you, Lord?" (Acts 9:5). But at the end of his life, tried by every adversity, he exclaimed in confidence, "I have kept the faith. Henceforth there is laid up for me the crown of righteousness, which the Lord, the righteous judge, will award to me on that Day" (2 Tim 4:7-8). Confidence always comes by immersing our faith in thick circumstance, serving Christ with our hands full, speaking truth into a gale of falsehood.

Living our confession will always result in maturity, and consistency is probably the best argument for convincing unbelievers. We acquire maturity not in dingy lecture halls but on crosses. In the hard circumstances of life, we are made strong by study and experience.

Thus in the next chapters I contrast the value of Christ's reason and modern-day absurdity. Next appear two chapters on why knowledge is important to Christians and how we acquire it. The central chapters of the book cover the role of miracles in faith, focusing on the miracles of Christ and the key miracle of all Christianity—the resurrection. The last chapter encourages us to embrace the "madness" of Christianity as the only refuge of meaning.

If I can, I would like once more to make friends of faith and reason and leave them sitting in peace in the same quiet life. For those who love Christ, perhaps this work will help make a reasonable faith the best kind of faith. It is to such a studied and courageous maturity that this book is dedicated.

This is the irrational season
When love blooms bright and wild.
Had Mary been filled with reason
There'd have been no room for the child.
Madeleine L'Engle

Promise me . . . that when I die only my friends shall stand
about my coffin, and no inquisitive crowd. See that no
priest or anyone else utter falsehoods at my graveside, when
I can no longer protect myself; and let me descend into
my tomb as an honest pagan.
Friedrich Wilhelm Nietzsche

The running battle of the star and clod
Shall run forever—if there be no God.
Herman Melville

2
A Carpenter's Reason

FOR CENTURIES A DEBATE has raged: Is Christ the supreme truth? Can he alone be internalized as final meaning? This debate between skeptics and believers emerged suddenly during Christ's lifetime. The quarrel began in the synagogue in Nazareth of Galilee (Lk 4:14-30). But it did not die there. For two thousand years it has set the reasoning of a carpenter against the scholars and doubters.

Carpenter or Christ?
The debate itself may seem a teapot tempest to moderns. It was a prosaic, Jewish debate; a trivial argument in a geographical nowhere. But the feud was crucial to the Jews of Nazareth. At the eye of the storm was a young Rabbi, newly ordained by God himself in the sun and the dust-brown fields. And here where the boy Jesus once played, the man Jesus stood to speak a truth that would resound forever.

Christ had come home to tell those who knew him best that

he was the Christ. He fulfilled in their hearing the words of Isaiah 61:1-2.

They doubted his declaration. The villagers who accused Jesus of lying did not think his announcement was preposterous. They all believed that one day the Messiah would come. Rather their furor was prompted by familiarity. The villagers knew Jesus too well! In Nazareth we meet that awful tendency of ours which reduces everything great. "Why, he is just a carpenter's son! We saw him growing up with his brothers James and Joses and Judas and Simon and his sisters, too. He's one of us. He's nothing supernatural!" We control things we cannot understand by giving them containable definitions. What the Nazarenes said that day was, "Nothing of worldwide significance can really happen here. We are ordinary people in an ordinary town. What makes this blue-collar worker think he's so special anyway?"

But the townsfolk could not imagine the vast reality beyond their small notions. They had him labeled, and labeling is a form of containment, a package in the mind. We like truth but only in controllable quantities. A Californian might reason: "I know the Golden Gate Bridge; I cross it twice each day. It has two piers and two cables. I have always known it that way; and, therefore, it can be no other."

Jesus was known in Nazareth—his height, his eyes, his coloring, his callused hands, his dark hair. His face and manners were common knowledge. It was unthinkable that this well-known villager would stand on a normal, sun-baked Sabbath and say, "The Spirit of the Lord is upon me, because he has anointed me to preach good news to the poor. He has sent me to proclaim release to the captives and recovering of sight to the blind, to set at liberty those who are oppressed, to proclaim the acceptable year of the Lord" (Lk 4:18-19).

"No," cried the townspeople. "You are the village timber-dresser. Joseph's boy. Yes, of course you are! That's all!"

It is difficult to call a well-known carpenter the Christ. Knowing him well, they chose the smaller modifiers: Jesus, son of Joseph, not Son of God! Carpenter, not Christ! Protesting that they knew him well, they proved they did not know him at all.

Tracking God with a Lantern

Those in Nazareth who thought him only a carpenter are gone by centuries. They died insisting that he was as mortal as themselves. But the issue must be redecided by each new generation. And those who hear of him in every era must continue to take one side or the other. Nero, Voltaire and Bertrand Russell chose to believe him only a carpenter. Paul, Augustine and Mother Teresa called him the Christ.

When any argument is intense the middle way is a no man's land. There were none in Nazareth that day who said, "Maybe carpenter, maybe Christ!" Everyone took sides. What is unexpected is the dogmatism of those in the carpenter camp. One would expect Christians to insist that Jesus is the Christ. But it is surprising to hear cynics fervently affirming "This is only Joseph's boy!" They study, live and die all to prove that Christ was a mere carpenter. If you ask them why they are so zealous in their negative evangelism, they say their carpenter theology is all in the interest of enlightenment, intellectual honesty, the advance of reason.

When the battle begins, Christians and Carpentarians fight with very different weapons. Christians bring their Bibles, visions, sound words and living experiences saying, "Now see here." Carpentarians bring their encyclopedias, calculators and data books replying, "You were saying?" The Carpentarians resemble Nietzsche's mad man who came into the marketplace on a sunlit day carrying a lantern which he thrust into every darkened niche and cried, "I seek God! I seek God!" Since he did not find God, he concluded that God was dead and the churches were nothing more than his tombs and sepulchers.

Carpentarians, like Nietzsche's mad man, usually use the wrong tools in their search for truth. You do not track God with a lantern and a coil of rope. Facts *are* empirical; you may therefore use lanterns to illuminate them and ropes to bind them when they are discovered. Christianity is a reality embedded deep in mystery. Its transforming truth is not discoverable by science alone.

Christianity is not without logic; but its greatest truth cannot be proved by logic alone. There are other categories of great meaning that elude logic. A man and a woman are said to be in love. Their love, real as it is, is hardly empirical. Love is not chemical or biological or animal or vegetable or mineral. Yet it exists. The best that the romantic lyricist can do to define it is to croon, "I don't know why I love you like I do; I don't know why; I just do." Carpentarians fall in love, accepting easily the riddle of romance. But in fury they question faith.

Christians accept faith in joy. They admit, "I do not know how faith and meaning exist—but I know they do. As Carpentarians must try to explain the issue of love, Christians must try to answer questions on faith.

In John 6, the Jews were upset because Jesus had just claimed to be the bread come down from heaven. But the skeptics ask, "Is not this Jesus, the son of Joseph, whose father and mother we know? How does he now say, 'I have come down from heaven?' " (Jn 6:42). He is certainly someone great for he has just divided the loaves among thousands. But he is not the Messiah!

Carpentarians get lost in procedure. Their conclusion comes only after they have applied all the methods of inquiry. It seems to them that Christians can't believe anything because they cannot defend it to the satisfaction of the skeptics. Logic always has the last word, even when it is empty.

A Tale of Faith

If the truth that Christians own is beyond reason, can they ever defend the reality of an unprovable faith? The best way to reason beyond reason is to argue from experience. Most Christians feel it is important to share their testimonies from time to time. A testimony is a tale of faith. It is the most dynamic, if subjective, evidence that a believer possesses.

Remember romantic love? Suppose a skeptic demands some evidence of romance. What we cannot argue from science we can argue from experience. We testify to romance. We protest that we are in love and have all the symptoms. We tingle when we are around a certain person; we perspire; we get butterflies in our stomach. The skeptic may say that while these can be measurable phenomena, they tell us nothing of love. In desperation, we point to the lipstick on our collar or the engagement ring and say, "See, here is the evidence."

"No," argues the skeptic, "These are only evidences of diamond mining or the cosmetic industry and do not conclusively prove that a condition of love exists." He is certainly a hard mind, yet he is right. Our best recourse is to wish our antagonist to fall in love. Once Cupid's arrows pierce him, his logic will go flat; then he will know that love really does exist.

Is it legitimate to give our testimony in defense of our faith? The psalmist defended truth on the basis of experience. "Taste and see," he challenged (Ps 34:8). Once Jesus had performed the miracle of the loaves, he claimed to be the bread of heaven. "I am the bread of life. Your fathers ate the manna in the wilderness, and they died. This is the bread which comes down from heaven, that a man may eat of it and not die. I am the living bread which came down from heaven; if any one eats of this bread, he will live for ever; and the bread which I shall give for the life of the world is my flesh" (Jn 6:48-51). However unreasonable it sounded, those who had tasted the loaves and fishes had to taste of faith to know its reality. Using the same logic, Jesus invited a Samaritan woman to taste the water of life and see if it wouldn't quench her thirst forever (Jn 4:13).

Experience can be a formidable foe even for the hard-line cynic. In John 9 a man born blind is healed. This ignites a controversy in the council of elders. They doubt Christ but are forced to admit that the man can see. The blind man was far more enthusiastic than Jesus' critics. The skeptics were dull to his experience. They could see that the blind man was healed but were reluctant to believe that Jesus was more than a man. They encouraged him to praise God and not Jesus, who was a sinner. (When we are beaten we face a great temptation to slur the victor.) "Whether he is a sinner, I do not know; one thing I know, that though I was blind, now I see" (Jn 9:35). The man, citing only his experience, makes such a brilliant defense that his adversaries cast him out.

Testimonies do not satisfy the Carpentarians' demand for logic, but they are powerful. Paul repeats his testimony three times in the book of Acts. Our experience with the truth may be subjective, but it cannot be refuted. It is hard to discount, especially when it is accompanied by further evidence of morality and ministry.

Scientific Sensations and Supernatural Signs

Some Christians, to compensate for hypocrisy, turn to "bigness" in relating their experience. It is a dramatic attempt to make Carpentarians sit up and take notice. The stop-the-music kind of testimony becomes flamboyant in an attempt to let experience shout down skepticism.

Then to the bigness of our testimony we add some kind of scientific sensation to support our conversion story. We beg archaeologists to dig up Sodom and Gomorrah. We call on the experts to find the rotting hulk of Noah's Ark on the frozen cliffs of Ararat. We do a computer and laser analysis of the Shroud of Turin. If only we could get the big evidence we need to accompany our simple testimony. This would be the big play! The grand slam!

The inward experience of Christ is apparently too ordinary to be respected by a doubting world. If only we had some dramatic spiritual vision like Fatima or Lourdes to overwhelm the doubters. We cry aloud, "God, speak to us as you once spoke to Paul in the desert lightning! Set Constantine's fiery cross blazing in the heavens once more. Please, God, could we borrow Elijah's chariot of flame to ride in to our university philosophy class for one day!"

Only a few in the history of Christianity could boast of such visions and revelations. Most have had to make their defense with less spectacular experiences. I suppose all Christians who have defended their faith to skeptics have pled for a little fire to hallow the humdrum. Young John Bunyan once tried to call down divine fire to dry up a mud puddle so he could have firsthand, visible evidence of the supernatural.

The world would find it easier to believe in the invisible God if only he would offer visible signs of his existence. Or, would they? Christ refused to give Herod a sign. Jesus knew it would not have convinced him for long. Christ knew signs were unnecessary to real faith. He also knew how futile they often were. When Jesus multiplied the loaves, the end product of the miracle was stupefaction and not faith.

The absence of supernatural "proofs" keeps Christianity from being a bargain-basement religion—a poor man's cabalism of mystifying events that get all the oohs and ahhs of a fireworks display. Fireworks are brilliant against the dark sky, but they are short-lived. And worse, they leave us in an inky blackness trying to remember the exact form of their brief but fiery etchings.

Drama too is unavailing. Jesus told the story of the rich man and Lazarus to demonstrate this. The rich man in hell was torn by an awareness of his unrepentant brothers who were yet alive. He asked Father Abraham to resurrect the beggar, Lazarus, and send him to his living kin to preach a sermon on the horrors of hell. But Abraham countered, "They have Moses and the prophets; let them hear them."

Still the rich man argued, "No, father Abraham; but if some one goes to them from the dead, they will repent."

But Abraham had the last word, "If they do not hear Moses and the prophets, neither will they be convinced if some one should rise from the dead" (Lk 16:19-31).

Suppose for a moment that Abraham had granted the rich man's wish and brought Lazarus back from the dead. Lazarus would have stalked into the family reunion of the surviving relatives saying, "I bear you greetings from your dead brother. He is in hell. He screams in pitiless torment night and day. It is his wish that you sell your villas, wardrobes and estates, and become charitable and loving, turning your lives over in service to the Almighty. This is the only way you can avoid his eternal sufferings."

Would his kinsfolk have listened to the resurrected Lazarus? It is doubtful. Ebenezer Scrooge may be the only person converted to altruism by ghosts from the past. Probably they would have argued like Scrooge that Lazarus's shade was a bit of "undigested beef" or an "old potato." Old visions in time degenerate into ghost stories. Years later the rich man's family would likely have laughed about the night they saw old Lazarus at the family reunion. They would have kept the lights high when they told of the event, but their lives would still be centered around the acquisition of things just like their dead, agonizing relative.

Practical Reasons

Paul argues for a less dramatic but more productive communication of our experience. "Faith comes from what is heard, and what is heard comes by the preaching of Christ" (Rom 10:17). Defending truth is best done by using ordinary speech and reason. We may imagine that our testimonies would go better if we divided seas while our adversaries focused their polaroid cameras in amazement. But people are impressed more deeply with something practical. Like the man born blind, we must understand that the direct effect Christ has on our lives is worth more than drama.

A new convert who was once an alcoholic came under fire by an agnostic demanding to know exactly how Christ changed water into wine. His chief concern was practical. "I do not know how or why Christ changed water to wine. I only know that in my case he did something far more useful: he changed my beer into furniture." The "use" of the truth we keep is ultimately more impressive than the "wow" of it.

Thus the carpenter's reason is always practical. Christ did not intend for Christianity to be a doctrinal gallery where our greatest dogmas were on display for admiration or debate. Rather, Christianity was to be a physician's black bag. Everything in the interest of good health is there. There are the tools to treat the major wounds of living, sterilizers for cleansing infected philosophies, Band-Aids for the little hurts that make up so much of life. The Sermon on the Mount is an exposé of the practical nature of Christ's teaching. Even his initial announcement of his Messiahship to the woman at the well was a statement on how practical and meaningful Christianity should be. Christianity was born to liberate the captives; it would cure the diseased; it would bring good news to the poor and the downtrodden.

Jesus' brother, James, once a Carpentarian, became a Christian after the resurrection. His letter, included in the New Testament, is a practical document. James believed that a gospel which did not warm the naked and nourish the starving laid no real claim to authenticity. "Faith apart from works is dead," said James (2:26). He is right. Any philosophy which only intrigues is worthless. The best thing to be said of Christianity is that besides being true, it also works!

Remember the miller in the fairy tale "Rumpelstiltskin"? It was enough for him that his daughter could spin straw into gold. It was a practical and useful talent. The miller was not even curious enough to inquire how his daughter started with bundles and ended with ingots. The "how" was not so important as the visible, spendable results.

Skeptics, however, are usually theoreticians. The fact that Christianity works will never be totally satisfactory to them. Someone will always want to know the schematics of atonement or wrangle over the genetics of the Virgin Birth. But discussion is the pastime of those that are well fed and at ease. When Jesus multiplied the loaves for this starving, rag-tag assembly, the penniless peasants ate. It may have been the first meal many of them had enjoyed in weeks. Here was a practical Messiah who served real bread with his sermons.

It was only when the crowd was filled that they became philosophical. The hungry rarely have time for high thoughts. Great revivals of hope are born in times of need. In seasons of abundance, warmed with bread and fish, men volley with cynicism and play with their doubts.

Doubt becomes a way of life just as faith does. Hard-core skeptics have often fallen in love with arguing as a lifestyle.

They don't want to be convinced by the practical nature of the Christian faith. Argumentation is their greatest joy. Becoming a Christian would eliminate the argument and ruin their fun.

The cry of Christians from century to century has been, "Jesus is Christ." To those who yell back across the trenches, crying, "No, he is only a carpenter," we must point to the issues of inner meaning. If the skeptics reply that we are to be pitied for our superstitions, let us ask them to show us the hope of their philosophies. If they argue that they are enlightened, let us ask if they have peace. If they say they know honesty, let us ask if they know truth.

At the person of Christ two roads diverge. Those on the barren road disappear over the horizon of time, muttering in hunger that he was only a carpenter. Those on the other road admit that they cannot answer all questions. Still they are on a pilgrimage to drive a certain stake in a promised destiny. And ever and anon they stop and cry for the overwhelming joy that fills them and spills over the brim of meaning, "He is the Christ!"

> *Dachau lost the dimension of reality*
> *in which alone man can exist as a human being.*
> *Man was nothing more than material, a matter which*
> *could be made from the production of soap.*
> **Johann Neuhauster**

King Arthur's apology for being man:
> *I suppose I had better go away and drown myself. I am*
> *cheeky, insignificant, ferocious, stupid and impolitic.*
> *It hardly seems to be worth our going on.*
> **T. H. White**

> *If there is no God, then everything is permitted.*
> **Fyodor Dostoevsky**

3
Against Absurdity

MEANINGLESSNESS THREATENS us everywhere. William March's unknown soldier, wounded and wallowing in the barbed wire was put to death by a kind German officer. As his eyes fluttered closed, the soldier said, "I have broken the chain. . . . I have defeated the inherent stupidity of life."[1] Is death the end of the empty routine? Certainly dying outside of Christ is not a triumph over existence. Death may be as void of hope as life.

Without Christ absurdity mocks all purpose. A universe without God is a black hole where all idealism is drawn into the dark maelstrom of our arrogance and lust for power. Erase God and whatever is, is moral. Tyranny is as right as love. Nuclear war is as wholesome as peace. Altruism is indulgence. Sacrifice is hedonism.

The legacy of nihilism is an insatiable hunger to affirm ourselves. Emptiness is the inheritance of those who walk away from the Holy One. Bleakness comes from substituting human glory for God's glory. Secular humanism always protests,

"Isn't it true that man has come a long way on his evolutionary climb from the amoeba to the stars? Since we cannot celebrate the fatherhood of God, may we not at least praise the creative courage of man who is ever moving upward in the lonely universe?" Elevating ourselves as the reason to believe in the future ends in arrogant narcissism.

How did we come to think so well of ourselves in the West? Though there is plenty of sweet food to eat, the mood at the table is sour. We smile but it is only a grinning pessimism.

Oddly, less prosperous times yielded more hope. Times of want and oppression frequently produced the poetry of optimism: Black slaves sang their joyous spirituals with the lash scars gleaming in ebony. Yet with far more freedom in these latter days, themes of oppression are common. Similarly, Christians under the persecution of the Caesars burned with apocalyptic optimism. Yet in our own era of abundance, some theologians have proclaimed God dead. Today, heavy with possessions, space-age men and women whimper themselves to sleep in their gilded dwellings of despair.

As the West moved from a religious world view to a secular one, God became more remote. Sir Richard Gregory expressed this trend in his own epitaph:

My grandfather preached the gospel of Christ,
My father preached the gospel of Socialism,
I preach the gospel of Science.[2]

God's greatness began to diminish as our understanding of the universe grew. Between Galileo and Carl Sagan, the universe expanded infinitely. In learning the universe's dimension, we microsized ourselves as well as God. The Inquisitor in Brecht's study of Galileo confessed:

My child, it seems that God has blessed our modern astronomers with imaginations. It is quite alarming! Do you know that the earth—which we old fogies supposed to be so large

—has shrunk to something no bigger than a walnut, and the new universe has grown so fast and prelates—and even cardinals—look like ants. Why, God Almighty might lose sight of a Pope![3]

Such scientific conclusions have driven us to the brink of despair, and existential philosophy has pushed us over. Secular evolution teaches that we came from nothing personal. And popular philosophy denies us life beyond our life span. We are headed nowhere. Having zeroes for both our origin and destiny, the only conclusion is that life is nothingness.

Our war against meaninglessness has uncovered a cache of weapons used in the struggle. We slash at senselessness with bourbons, cocaine, open sexuality and new cars, bigger boats and more spacious houses. We buy psychiatry and contemplate the mysticism of the East. We titillate our fascination with cabalism, bare our souls in therapy and answer the cold night of being with giddy laughter.

Some of those trapped in the desperation of nothingness have tried the popular forms of Christianity and turned away disappointed. The church, which should produce meaning, sometimes produces only a sterile, institutional business. Crying out for meaning, disappointed seekers are offered only a committee presidency or a chance to usher. Statisticians coldly observe that the rate of church growth barely keeps up with the growth of suicide.

Thus comes that haunting question that Christians must answer or accept their own irrelevancy: Does Christianity contain substantial meaning? The frightened world is asking, "Is anybody home in the universe?" Those outside the church desperately appeal to those inside for answers. While they yearn to know how they should live, more deeply they desire to discover why. As Nietzsche said, "He who has a *why* to live can bear with almost any *how*."

Reason to Live, Reason to Die

Victor Frankl escaped the horrors of the Auschwitz death camp determined to deal with the why of existence. During his imprisonment he saw life stripped to the stark minimum. With little reason to hope, he forged a philosophy of hope. He observed that those under rigorous deprivations abandoned all interest in sex (contrary to Freud). The tortured did not pursue any hope of power (the preoccupation of Alfred Adler). One thing alone survived in the death camp . . . hope. Meaning lived within the gaunt inmates of Auschwitz. Never did they quit believing no matter how little reason they had for hope.

Victor Frankl has alluded to a survey taken in France in which eighty-nine per cent of the people polled admitted that everybody needs something to live for. Also, sixty-one per cent of those interviewed said that there was somebody or some issue for which they were willing to die. Jean-Baptiste Clamence in Albert Camus's *The Fall,* did not rate God very high as something for which one would die. But the apostle Paul would roundly disagree "For to me to live is Christ, and to die is gain" (Phil 1:21).

While Frankl, being Jewish, did not say that ultimate meaning is Christ, he did say it is spiritual. His therapy is not psychotherapy (mind therapy) but logotherapy, that is, meaning therapy. Logotherapy, says Frankl, dares to enter the spiritual side of human existence.[4] Interpreting this statement in a Christian context is our only hope of confronting absurdity redemptively. Only by acting in faith can we demonstrate that there is a why to the question of life.

How desperate is the hunger to believe, to find a real reason to live! The most rigid determinists from time to time would trade their hopeless dogma for meaning. Even those who view the universe as a machine without God will sometimes reach for love or offer a prayer beyond the earshot of their peers. When Lenin finally took control of Russia, those standing near him said he traced the sign of the cross in the air before him.

The Marquis de Sade could argue convincingly that everything was chemically determined, even morality; therefore, any happenstance was right and just. Yet during his confinement in Charenton, he complained about his "unjust" treatment by the jailers. He spent hours pouring over his wife's letters, although according to his own argument, they were just the chemical etchings of an autonomous and absurd universe. Is it possible that de Sade himself was reaching for a why for life?

Existentialism has been brutal in its war against human meaning. Jean-Paul Sartre and Albert Camus, French existentialists, believed that while life is entirely absurd, we can only become meaningful by the exercise of our will. We authenticate ourselves by deciding. In choosing to be moral or charitable, one may become real in an illusionary world. Sartre's play *No Exit* is a picture of humanity locked in an absurd universe, and while living must go on, it goes on pointlessly.

Jaspers, the Swiss existentialist, speaks of finding our authenticity through what he calls the final experience. This is any experience of such an impressive nature that it gives one the assurance that he is really there. Without such an experience every person's life is nothing and buried in bleak meaninglessness.

Contemporary literature—plays, screen plays and novels —have echoed themes of human hopelessness. This quote from Henry Miller reflects the typical mood of such writing:

> There are always too many rotten pillars left standing, too much festering humanity for man to bloom. The superstructure is a lie and the foundation is a huge, quaking

fear. . . . Who that has a desperate, hungry eye can have the slightest regard for these existing governments, laws, codes, principles, ideals, ideas, totems and taboos? Out of nothingness arises the sign of infinity; beneath the everlasting spirals slowly sinks the gaping hole . . . I see that behind the nobility of [man's] gestures there lurks the spectre of the ridiculousness of it all. . . . He is not only sublime but absurd.[5]

The doctrine of the absurd has also been advanced by the modern artists. Later surrealists and the entire Dada school painted and sculpted life as essentially meaningless. Poets like artists got into the act. One of the poems of Dadist, Kurt Schwitters, contains this verse:

Bumm bimbimm bamm bimbimm
Bumm bimbimm bamm bimbimm
Bumm bimbimm bamm bimbimm
Bumm bimbimm bamm bimbimm[6]

The poem is longer than this but enough is quoted to convey the empty rhymes of absurdists.

Many Christians believe that God may actually be stalking us to offer meaning in the Person of his Son. In Francis Thompson's "The Hound of Heaven" God follows us through the existential deserts, extending the overflowing cup with refreshing love.

The Hound of Heaven pursues us, and we are disinterested lovers, consistently ignoring God. Our hunger for meaning has more often turned us toward materialism, power and fame.

When secularism has run its course, it often disconnects us from our conscience. We then have no obligation to the mechanistic universe that produced us. We are evolution's best, set free to manage our own ends. No wonder that Johann Neuhauster wrote in his own letter concerning the concentration camp at Dachau:

Here a collective sadism was let loose and spat into the face of men, beat and kicked them without inhibitions. Here inhumanity became the law of man. It is fatal to fall into the hands of men. . . .

The break with God and Christ was the beginning which led to the perfect and legally sanctioned murder.[7]

If Neuhauster is right, to stop believing in God paves the way to the annihilation of life. To believe in God, then, is essential to the continuance of life. In the face of skeptical intellectuals this may seem naive. They accuse us of being simplistic if we set forth Jesus and the Bible as the antidote to cultural death.

But we who are Christians ought to ache for all the scholars and artists who are fettered to absurdity. Christians should cry out for atomic physicists who can smash atoms but do not understand that they are loved. One wonders if Dada artists or existential philosophers have ever been told that God loves them. Informed Christians, under the compulsion of sheer love, must be willing to bear witness to hungry intellectuals.

The Meaning of Mystery

From the very outset, those who wish to probe the Bible for meaning must fix one point clearly. Just as logic is related to knowledge, so mystery is related to faith. The entire success of the venture for meaning is dependent on this. Those who seek, and read the Bible as they would their chemistry text, will find nothing.

In the *Brothers Karamazov* Smerdyakov refuses to believe the Bible's account of creation because of what seems to him an inconsistency. Light was created on the first day, according to Genesis but the sun was not created until the fourth day. Smerdyakov, reasoning that light comes from the sun, loses confidence in the whole scriptural account. Immediately following his attempt to harmonize that inconsistency he is taken with his first epileptic seizure, a disease that was to follow him the rest of his life.

Any person who tries to force his view of the Scripture into logic, like Smerdyakov, is destined to end up in jangling, intellectual epilepsy. Salvation is God's alternative to meaningless living and dying. God offers this to everyone without all the explanation and procedural data. Knowing the great why of life, we are to trust God with the how.

We are the children of the technocracy and cannot live easily with unsolved mysteries. We must understand or live in despair because the mystery will not declare itself. We live under the illusion that if we could understand more we would be happier. How foolish!

Faith and mystery are codependent. Eliminate either and you have destroyed the other. Faith cannot be faith once it is fully explained and the mystery is gone. God acts in ways that will not comfortably nestle into human gray matter. Suppose for a moment that some Christians were able to solve all the mysteries of God. Would they not lord it over all the rest of us who had not managed their understanding? Would they not be prone to boast, "Come see my little God and the graphs that chart his thoughts."

To fight against the mystery of faith is foolish. The mystery of faith contains within it a reply all its own to the skeptical world it encounters. Bible-believing Christians cannot prove the existence of God by using the Bible, but neither can atheists answer all of their own questions. Which question is easier to answer, the mystery of the Trinity or the origin of the universe without God?

Once the atheist Robert Ingersoll met the great Congregational pastor Henry Ward Beecher. Ingersoll was renowned for his militant unbelief and his cutting debates with the pious, where he nearly always managed to "prove" there was no God.

They once met in Beecher's study in Plymouth Church in Boston. A part of the decor of the study was a beautifully made celestial globe—an attractive piece of art, meticulously constructed. Ingersoll scrutinized it and said, "Henry, that's magnificent! Who made it?" The pastor answered with sparkling wit, "Why, Robert, nobody made it; it just happened."

Ingersoll and Beecher represent two poles, faith and antifaith. Some, like Ingersoll, have a know-it-all attitude toward Christian mystery. But they cannot answer all questions satisfactorily. There are great questions about creation, destiny and meaning they can't answer. Neither can they answer many questions about personality, psyche or guilt. For such the universe itself is there, but without meaning.

Perhaps the major difference between Christians and skeptics is this: Christians accept the mysterious God and the universe is solved. Atheists deny God and must, therefore, live in a mysterious universe.

But the greatest barrier to skeptics' salvation is the failure of Christians to confront doubt with bold faith. We have kept the Christ in the crypt. The world is suspicious of all mention of God out of the proper gothic context. Thus Jesus, like a medieval Bible, seems chained to the church.

St. Peter on his way into the city passed a cripple in a cranny of the city wall. In compassion and, more importantly, in the sunlight and fresh air of the outside world, he said to the man, "In the name of Jesus!" Today the cripple would say, "Please, not here . . . everyone is staring. Let's do it some other way— I'll meet you on Easter in church."

What happened that day was a thing of beauty. The lame man walked, even leaped. It all happened because the name of Jesus was spoken in courage to a hopeless soul. Flinging his paraphernalia in the ecstasy of his wholeness, he ran.

He ran because it seemed the thing to do when he had never

done it before. He ran because Peter had caused him to hear a new inner Christ who set him free to be whole. He heard this inner Christ cry, "Run child, let them know that there is power in Jesus' name. Run if you love God. Let them doubt that your mind has strength, but not your ankles. Run! *Run! RUN!*"

How desperately the church needs to learn that there is power in the name of Jesus spoken in the sunlight. That name can still set the dumb to singing and cripples sprinting through a host of cynics.

Jesus lived freely in the world of the Caesars, striding with power and dignity, healing and meaning. Only in these latter times have we subdued him and forced him to live in the dark to preside over our solemn and candlelit assemblies. Like a captured animal, the liturgical Christ roars against our euphonies. Pacing nervously, he longs to escape the church house and meet the needs of the suffering and the damned who lie beyond. He is protesting our artificial categories of the sacred and the secular. The world is his and he belongs in all of it.

Christians are called to participate in his ministry of meaning. He has sent us to go boldly and preach optimism in an absurd world. The impact of the meaning we know will be for some a release from captivity. Christ is the reason to live —for an individual or a world.

A Detonation of Life

One day Helen Keller's teacher placed in her hand the key that was to unlock her silent blackness. Neither hearing nor seeing from infancy, she had no way to learn sign language nor to communicate with signs or symbols. She had been touching hundreds of objects but there was no way to know what they were without sight and sound. Her teacher took her down a familiar path to the well-house where someone was drawing water. Her teacher let the cold water run over her one hand and in sign language spelled into the other W-A-T-E-R. Suddenly Helen felt a symbol of something stirring in the gray darkness of her consciousness. Suddenly she came alive. She had a single word composed of five letters. But that single word of five letters set her free at last from the dumb prison of herself. Suddenly she knew that like water everything in the world had a name. She left the well-house alive with the new possibility of becoming a real, communicating person in a world that opened to her all at once.

Young Helen might have appeared strange to any who saw her in ecstasy, but she was athrill with what she called a detonation. A silent, dumb absurd world was exploding with singing life, and she was in the middle of it all.

Christ has been the detonation for many lives. In fact, my own testimony of him would be one like Helen Keller's: Christ for me gave a new light and joy, and all the world I knew at last made sense because of him. Life for me is new every morning because Christ ever makes all things new.

There are still millions devoid of meaning—starved people who live in a plain world going nowhere. It is time for a detonation. These need to know that with Christ, life becomes bearable: yes, and more than bearable, hopeful. Christ and emptiness, like fire and water, cannot occupy the same space at one time. He stands at the door and knocks. Wise people quickly lift the latch to welcome him—the only alternative to absurdity.

I had rather be a toad
And live upon the vapour of the dungeon,
Than keep a corner in the thing I love
For others' uses.
William Shakespeare

For even saintly folk will act like sinners
Unless they have their customary dinners.
Bertolt Brecht

Men undertake to be spiritual, and then become ascetic;
or endeavoring to hold a liberal view of comforts
and pleasures of society, they are soon buried in the world,
and become slaves to its fashions.
Horace Bushnell

4
What Matter?

WHAT WE KNOW IS what we own. This is a difficult concept. We do not often think of knowledge as something we possess and prize. Usually we think that to have is to own.

Why is knowledge valued so little? Because material ownership permeates every molecule of our thinking. Materialism has become the religion of the West. Man in secular science is himself only part of the material universe. In all the cosmos there seem to be only two kinds of material—material that is owned and material that owns. The owners are called persons. The owned is called stuff. Of all the labels we in the West cherish, the word *owner* seems most important. Nearly everyone seems to have a need to say, "This particular stuff is mine."

Occasionally here and there we hear of a Trappist monk or a guru who gives up all desire for stuff and lives his days as a stuffless person. Most of us, however, never seem to understand how people manage to give it "all" up so easily.

Like people, nations play the ownership game. Countries

may brag that all the substance between the river on the north and the mountains on the south is theirs. Conquistadors once planted Spanish flags all over South America claiming the land as a possession of their king. The battles for possession sometimes rage for centuries. Perhaps the most grandiose symbol of possessiveness in recent days was the planting of the American flag on the moon. While presumably Americans would not say they own lunar real estate, they would never permit any subsequent flag-planters to say that they owned it either.

With the exception of such things as oxygen, oceans, sunlight and migratory birds, everything in our world is either a possessor or a possession. Therefore, many philosophies have arisen concerning our relationship to stuff. Karl Marx, for example, taught that only by an equitable division of all material goods among all people could life have meaning for everyone.

The church too has become a victim of materialism. For centuries Christianity was largely the pastime of the poor who only dreamed of being wealthy in heaven. But wealth is no longer just the destiny of believers in the West; it is their status quo. To the poor of the world, the Christ who once came in poverty now seems to ride a golden calf. Indeed, it must be difficult to tell if we now worship the rider or his mount. They wonder if we follow a Christ who traded his healing touch for the Midas touch.

Intangible Substance
Jesus, however, has done nothing of the sort. He taught that things were not as they appeared. Material things which seem substantial are subject to canker, decay, rust and dissolution. True stuff, on the other hand, was not tangible and marketable. In fact, one could acquire true stuff only in certain instances by selling all he had (Mt 19:21).

Christ taught that only as we lay up treasure in heaven will we be able to know meaning. As long as we continue to insist that materialism is the route to meaning, we will be lost in our striving after these things which can never commend us to God.

In the Sermon on the Mount, Christ taught that true stuff could not be labelled "mine" and locked in safety-deposit boxes. The real possessions were laid up beyond the planet (Mt 6:19-20), for all earthy material is transient (Jas 5:2). Jesus' classic illustration on the nature of true stuff was the rich fool (Lk 12:16-21) who amassed an earthly fortune but departed life bereft.

The materialists, in contrast to Christ, have implied that real estate, stocks and bonds, mercantile items are the true stuff. No, argues Christ; spiritual understanding is true stuff and the Spirit of God enables us to become as enduring as the heavens themselves.

Greed is the stepchild of a materialist world view. When we are owned by greed we gradually care less and less for mystery and knowledge. We soon find all our love for eternal things eroded by a compelling lust for material things.

Greed is nothing more than stuff hunger, and this greed has not only led us into lasciviousness with our resources, it has raped the earth with consumerism. The ecology movement is a backlash to the greedy seizing of natural resources for corporate profit.

Ecologists do a great deal of good. But while the preservation of the material world is important to all of us, ultimate value lies beyond matter in spirit. Christ taught us to not love too dearly anything material, natural or financial, for nothing is to be profited by gaining the whole world and losing your own soul (Mt 16:26).

Ecology deals with our stewardship of the world. It acts in

the interest of general human ownership of a perishing world. Individual greed, on the other hand, makes everybody suffer. The rich suffer from wanting more; the poor suffer from having less and craving more. An old song well expressed the misery inherent in greed:

Ask the rich man, he'll confess,
Money can't buy happiness.
Ask the poor man, he don't doubt,
That he'd rather be miserable with than without.

Communism idealistically holds a desire to eliminate the misery of materialism. Marx protested that capitalistic greed had built a grotesque world. His idealism degenerated, however, into forms of government which have actually persecuted many of the economically downtrodden. Still, who could argue with what Marx observed: history is frequently the story of those gone mad with greed? Ours is a world where Venetian doges oppress the poor and Czars ride their gilded sleighs to their grand mansions through Moscow's intolerable slums.

Not Stones but Souls

Christ established his church to counter a life built on greed for silver and gold and ordinary riches. But "the church" has become architectural in our thinking—a building where believers meet. How false this is! The church is the body of Christ —composed not of stones but of souls. But contemporary churches do seem to be gilded temples, with expanded pledge drives and imported fixtures. They still claim to be in business for a penniless carpenter, but their budgets belie their values. Preaching that human souls are the real stuff, their boards of investors buy apartment complexes and football stadiums. Indeed, few churches in the West are able to say with the apostle Peter in the first century, "Silver and gold have I none."

A materialistic Christianity infects the capitalistic empires of certain television evangelists and concert artists. In the huckstering of their ministry, many have become wealthy, leaving only disillusioned disciples in their wake.

In James Michener's novel *Hawaii* the John Whipple family arrived in the Hawaiian Islands to practice Christian compassion. Soon they saw how the Islands (and themselves) could profit from opening a general store to sell consumer goods. Within a few generations the Whipples owned a great many stores and other holdings. Their noble idealism of teaching the heathen about Christ was lost in their own financial success. Likewise, the church too often treasures what stockbrokers endorse. She drones on about eternal values and her dead eyes only sparkle when she begins talking of properties and bank notes and certificates of deposit.

It is said that when the Communists were meeting in Russia to decide how to take over the world, the bishops were meeting down the street to decide what colors their vestments ought to be for the various liturgies. One wonders what the bishops preached after they had decided which of their costly vestments to wear. In their ermine-trimmed capes, did they tell the student rabble that the Bolsheviks sinned in seeking only material answers to social problems, when, after all, the true stuff was spiritual?

In our own country the church has often catered to a strange brand of Calvinism. Adam Smith, that delightful alias who wrote *The Money Game,* said, "Bishop Lawrence . . . was J. P. Morgan's preacher, and on a Sunday he would look down at the assembled Wall Street tycoons in individually endowed pews and say, 'Godliness is in league with riches; it is only to the moral man that wealth comes. Material prosperity makes the nation sweeter, more joyous, more unselfish, more Christlike.' "[1] Smith calls this "Faith according to the Closing Quotations." There can be little doubt as to what Bishop Lawrence's parishioners thought true stuff was.

Perhaps the dichotomy of the church and her values might be summed up by an ivory nativity scene (kept most of the year under lock and key). Here in glittering expense is captured the birth of the poor peasant, Jesus—valuable idols which suggest that earth's greatest possessions are not valuable idols.

Elton Trueblood has given us a painful look at our double allegiance at Christmas: "If we are inclined to dispute the existence of materialism in the West, all that is required to convince us of its reality is a careful study of advertisements, particularly at Christmas. In preparation for the birthday of Him who had no where to lay His head, we are urged to buy for the wife a forty-thousand-dollar necklace or, for a couple, matching airplanes marked His and Hers."[2] Christmas would not be a good time for the church to argue that she represents another set of values from those held by the rest of the world.

The traditional church stands little chance of preaching a doctrine of true stuff and attracting any serious disciples with it. Like St. Francis, we need to forsake our affluence for we cannot cling to it and convince anyone, even ourselves, that we operate by Christ's values. In the current materialistic milieu, we must stand amidst our greedy peers guarding their goods, and say, "The things of the spirit are mine! Gaze on my invisible realities: the knowledge of God, the possession of meaning."

A Life (and Death) of Inner Wealth

Death makes a comedy of the discrepancy between what we say we love and what we really love! Dying is the end of all ownership, and if owning is life's greatest station, then death is life's greatest tragedy. Death can never be victorious to the committed materialist. It is rather a bleak disinheritance.

The death of a contemporary missionary, Jim Elliot, stands in contrast. At the time of his martyrdom he was a man without material substance, at least very much of it. Yet, he had amassed an impressive amount of ministry to human misery. A Wall Street tycoon might have been unimpressed if Elliot had said, "There are my holdings: the knowledge of God, time invested for Christ's kingdom, dreams energized by God's Spirit, love for my assassins." Yet after his death there settled on the world the strange aura of victory. He was, indeed, a man of wealth. His wife titled her book on his life and death *Through Gates of Splendor*.

I remember the news release from my childhood and the thrilling challenge it brought to me as an adolescent. I saw the passing of this poor missionary as that of a truly wealthy man. He had written just before he died, "He is no fool who gives what he cannot keep, to gain what he cannot lose."

Dying is not the only way to demonstrate our true substance. It must also be done by sacrificial living. We will have to accord the materialists this: having does indeed make them happy. One has only to note the elation of a sweepstakes winner or a recent heir to see the rapture of having. By this same logic, believers in Christ can demonstrate that they really have something only if their inner wealth excites them as if they were sweepstakes winners. Possessing every treasure should mark a life with joy.

St. Teresa called sour Christians "frowning saints." Frowning saints might say with scowling conviction that Christ has given them much. But who, indeed, would want their inner substance when it produces such an unhappy face? Christians who enjoy life and live with a great deal of joy will make others envious of their inner holdings. Remember the robbers who fell upon St. Francis and took his clothes from him and set him free? Imagine their surprise to hear him singing in the snow!

It was hard to rob St. Francis. He didn't have the kind of

wardrobe that a self-respecting bandit would wear. He had no money. The bread tied at his belt was half-eaten by birds. It would have been impossible to steal his horse: he had not owned a steed since his days as a nobleman. All of his assets were tied up in prayers, sermons and the kissing of untouchables. Still, his poverty was clothed with the joy of a song in a drift of snow. As one of the martyrs once said: "Joy is the most infallible proof of the presence of God." We are not a having people but a knowing people. We know the reality of spiritual wealth. The knowledge of God is the root of joy.

A Hunger to Know Christ

Learning the reality of the world of the spirit always supposes a life of study. We must pledge ourselves to the task of prayer and meditation. Yet our churches are frantic, busy places which keep their converts so involved that they leave little time to study. Modern evangelicalism nursed on revivalism and gospel music has been a mood-centered movement. This adoration has spawned a kind of giddy populism that speaks sweetly of Jesus but does not always appear intelligent. There is no hunger to know, only to feel Christ.

For the most part, current gospel heroes know only a little about the Bible and most of that knowledge is expressed in solely devotional terms. Any sense of the critical, historical or literary value of Scripture is missed.

Here and there, however, there are students of Scripture who are both disciplined and courageous. They have studied the Bible and become informed about the arts and sciences. Their knowledge of the Bible grows in two directions. They study the Bible devotionally and this issues in praise and worship. But they also study the Bible critically, learning the history of those movements and nations out of which Scripture came.

In the discipline of learning and out of the time spent with God, serious students of the Bible become usable weapons in the battle for understanding. They reject the common view of materialists that to *own* much is to *be* much. They have, however, developed a kind of greed. They have become ravenous for inwardness. They long for union with Christ. They grow in anticipation of that world where Christ lives in fullness—for there is his treasure stored. They may have little wealth here and now, but they are rich in a land where neither moth nor rust can corrupt, and thieves cannot break through and steal. In the confidence that comes from such assets, they walk through the snow in joy.

We are not here concerned with hopes or fears, only with the truth as far as our fear allows us to discern it.
Charles Darwin

*Things take indeed a wondrous turn
When learned men do stoop to learn.*
Bertolt Brecht

Thou hast studied thyself but into a dark and damnable ignorance, if thou have labored for much learning only to prove that thou canst not be saved.
John Donne

5
The Student of Christ

DISCIPLINE IS THE armor of faith. Without it, Christianity is only a set of creeds, and Christians walk their world exposed to harsh circumstances. I am unable to forget Cardinal Wolsey's words in Shakespeare's *Henry VIII,* "Had I but served my God with half the zeal I served my king, he would not in mine age have left me naked to mine enemies."[1] Only Christians who commit themselves to study and prayer can stand before their enemies in confidence. It is not always possible to win every one of our battles with the world, but with better spiritual discipline, we position ourselves for victory.

Instead of standing naked before Satan, Paul counseled us to put on the whole armor of God (Eph 6:11). There is a glorious confidence in knowing that we have a sure answer. Having disciplined ourselves we are able to give to everyone who asks a reason—an *intelligent* reason—for the hope that is in us (1 Pet 3:15). Only from a life of study and prayer can we turn aside the critics who charge that we are naive and overserious.

Matthew Arnold wrote of our predicament in *The Scholar Gypsy*. He said the believers of his day appeared to be

Light half-believers of our casual creeds,
Who never deeply felt, nor clearly will'd,
Whose insight never has borne fruit in deeds,
Whose vague resolves have never been fulfill'd.
For whom each year we see
Breeds new beginnings, disappointments new;
Who hesitate and falter life away,
And lose tomorrow the ground won today.

Learning can be a heavy burden, but being committed to it is the only way to stop our loss of ground.

New converts are first drawn to the church by the love of Christ. Many, however, soon develop a love for church politics. Church, which is at first a place to meet God, becomes a place to socialize. Its caucuses are coffee klatches and committee luncheons. New converts soon learn the art of linking Christ with softball and potluck dinners. They learn the art of climbing the church's political structures, placing themselves at last in nomination for congregational moderator. Their disciplined pursuit of God and the Bible are dropped. They trade a difficult discipleship for a religious image.

The Word and the World
The call to follow Christ is both a call to study the Bible and to know our world. As we study Christ, we must learn all we can about the great inequities of our world and minister to the oppressed. Our desire to help will be hidden in this truth: because it is *his* world, it is *our* world too.

If we seek the heart of Christ, we will seek to bridge the gap between need and study. It is right to meet the physical needs of those around us. Hunger must be answered with bread, disease with healing. But our concern for outer needs must never displace an equal concern for inner needs. Humanism cares deeply, but only about the physical side of the human plight. Dostoevsky said that humanism can be a form of atheism, for it focuses so intently on our material woes that it rarely gets around to dealing with our spiritual woes. Evangelism gets scrubbed by social concern.

At times, however, we Christians have overreacted to this by letting the fear of the taint of humanitarianism keep us from being human. We emphasize only the bread of life, rushing to save eternal souls with too little thought of saving the present age. We study the great missions passages of the Bible, hastily reading past Matthew 25:31-46 or James 2:15-17.

Intense zeal distorts nearly every other need and value system. Any cause which narrows to a white-hot laser beam sees only that tiny section of reality. Zeal has little peripheral vision.

Evangelism often cares fervently but narrowly. Not only does our missionary zeal pass by great fields of human need, it also blinds us to much of the beauty of art that surrounds us. It is a tragedy when people die without Christ. But it is also a tragedy when zeal for Christ shuts the mind down to wider learning because art and education in general seem a waste of time when placed beside the urgent business of saving souls. Sunday to Sunday we learn the words and the spirit of the great revival choruses but never seriously sample Tchaikovsky or Beethoven or even current Broadway repertoires. Most of us are not intentionally anti-Beethoven. We have just been too busy with merchandizing the greater truth of Christ. There is little time left for knowing the wider world.

Further, we have been stigmatized by our devotion to austerity. When our self-denial becomes rigorous, it appears stingy. When doctrine becomes stingy, it gets heavy with rules. Tight-fisted blue laws produce a frowning piety. This self-denial becomes a merit badge for those who give all. Proud that we are movieless, tobaccoless and pokerless, we usually appear joyless.

We sometimes mark our cultural poverty with otherworldly language. In the words of a popular hymn,

My Father is rich in houses and lands,
He holdeth the wealth of the world in his hand;
Of rubies and diamonds, of silver and gold,
His coffers are full, he has riches untold.
I'm a child of the King. . . .

While it is proper to lay up treasures in heaven, we must take this world seriously. Old hymnals often include a song which declares that this world is not my home. I'm just a-passing through. This attitude has kept us passing through this world en route to the next. Small wonder that skeptics have asked flippantly, "Christians have been around for two thousand years. Why in two thousand years could they not produce a world without the Gestapo or the Mafia?" The answer to this challenge is to participate in our world, not just to pass through.

In this participation, we shall have to move away from a purely devotional walk with Christ. We will have to study his Word and our world at the same time. We must enter the marketplace and argue intelligently the truth of God. Christianity is not only militant against sin, but also against ignorance and bad information. Truth of all kinds—spiritual or philosophical—must be defended. There are some who say they will not argue over religion for it is a private matter. But when anyone degrades our mates, we quickly rise, refusing to let the slur pass unchallenged. We do not respond, "I never argue about my wife. My wife is a private concern." What nonsense!

Similarly, there is no valid love of truth that will not defend it. We sometimes look on our creeds with reverence. But if faith has any value to us, there will come strong moments when we cry like Luther, "Here I stand. I can do no other."

Besides studying God's truth and defending it, we must also know the opposition. This cannot be done by focusing only on Scripture. The cynics subdue us not because they know the Bible but because they know art, philosophy, science and history.

Living in the great knowledge explosion of our day, the average Christian reads little. This ignorance leaves him incapable of defending his faith. This is a world of learning, of sight, sensation and sound. Dare we run a blind, deaf course to a cultural coma?

We must not sleep through this revolution. We need to read what our world is thinking as we, with them, rocket into the future. We need to learn what the philosophers are saying, the musicians are composing, the artists are painting, the authors are writing. And we need to learn in a disciplined way to formulate an intelligent world view.

To Stand

Before we can argue in strength, we will have to believe in ourselves. We have lost our intellectual self-respect and fear the scholars of this world. Too long we have allowed them to insinuate that we are incapable of good thinking. Christians who think they are culturally inferior cannot manage a convincing defense of their faith. We must stand up to intellectual arrogance with firm replies. We are not inferior. We need to speak loudly in the dignity of our discipleship. We are the defenders of his cross, and we must give secular scholars a bold demonstration of our self-esteem.

There is also an unfounded idea that as Christians learn more they abandon their faith. We need to stand against that idea. Conservative Christianity is not an intellectual stopover in the process of becoming a mature unbeliever. Fully understanding our world, we yet believe, and the better we are enlightened, the better we can answer its criticisms.

The danger of learning is that while it eliminates ignorance, it can foster arrogance. Intellectual pride turned inward does not defend the faith; it divides it. Uppity religion, gilded with tradition, has looked at revivalism with scorn. The high-church snub has been felt by low-status churchgoers. Faithful Pentecostals must weary of being told how many of the American presidents were Episcopalian.

While Christian education has helped put ignorance to flight, it has also given rise to religious status. Every defender of the faith must realize that there are no second-class citizens in God's kingdom.

Liberal Christians often boast of the excellence of their understanding, but they seem to lack zeal in missions. Conservative believers, while less knowledgeable, seem to be the only Christians with the stamina to change the world. Ultimately, missions and evangelism are the best evidence of obedience to Christ, whose last command was to take his gospel to the world. A wise missionary once said there is no use taking a lamp to Indonesia that will not burn at home. If our emphasis on education takes the heart out of John 3:16, we cannot claim to be either wise or learned.

Our fight for missionary integrity is as important as our need to know all we can about our world. But we cannot be satisfied with either/or. We must have both/and. We must study widely and preach Christ as our only hope.

To Risk

Preaching openly is risky. Paul was not sure that he would win his case on Mars Hill. He did, in fact, lose. But not totally. He gained "Dionysius . . . and a woman named Damaris and others" (Acts 17:34). Paul was an intellect, and true intellect can never be snubbed. The Athenian thinkers who had collided cerebrums with the apostle could not call him stupid simply because they disagreed with him. These intellectuals may have felt themselves superior to Paul, but their superiority could not blunt his argument. Paul was not ignorant. He reasoned from a studied base and they felt the power of his learning as he spoke.

The arena of Paul's defense was as important as its content. It takes courage to have open dialog. Karl Jaspers is no doubt right when he says, "If the churches dared . . . to put themselves in jeopardy, the word would be credible everywhere, everyday, on the lips of priests and theologians."[2] But we seldom have the courage to risk openly. We are too afraid of appearing naked in a day of grace. We have thus been reluctant both to defend and to acknowledge our faith.

The Gospels contain the story of a woman who had an issue of blood. She once approached Jesus in the press of a crowd and was healed by touching the hem of his garment. She must have reveled in her cure. But she also enjoyed the anonymity of it. After touching him, she tried to slip away in the crowd. But Christ did not permit her to evade her responsibility to acknowledge her healing: "Who touched me?" he asked. In the anonymity of our salvation, he still asks, "Who touched me?" If salvation is valuable, we must acknowledge it. Finding the courage to do so, we shall one day be able to defend it.

There are times when it is easy to be open about our faith and times when it is not. Demas, Paul's beloved missionary friend, could not be brave because of the perilous risk of exposure. It is with pain that the apostle wrote, "Demas, in love with this present world, has deserted me" (2 Tim 4:10). Defending the gospel might have been fatal to Paul. Demas was not up to that kind of pressure.

In Dostoevsky's novel about the famous Russian brothers,

Ivan Karamazov is on the witness stand to testify in behalf of his brother, Dmitri, falsely convicted of the murder of his father. The strain under which Ivan had been living caused him to go mad at the critical moment of testimony. Although Ivan was the only one in the courtroom with the knowledge to save Dmitri, he babbled incoherently and Dmitri was lost.

Perhaps the insane Ivan is the fearful reflection of so many Christians. We have been asked by God to take the witness stand for only we have the information that can save. But our testimony often comes out garbled—by personal experience and emotion. We have studied our world so little that we lack a profound awareness of the human predicament.

Time itself is often in the way of our defense. In our harried preoccupation with daily life, we cannot find some little space to set forth our testimony. Tolstoy wrote of our tendency to minimize faith by maximizing the routine.

I well remember the second time madness seized me. It was when Auntie was telling us about Christ. She told her story and got up to leave the room. But we held her back.

"Tell us more about Jesus Christ!" we said.

"I must go," she replied.

"No, tell us more, please!" Mitinka insisted and she repeated all that she had said before. She told us how they crucified him, how they beat and martyred him, and how he went on praying and did not blame them.

"Auntie, why did they torture him?"

"They were wicked."

"But wasn't He God?"

"Be still—it is nine o'clock; don't you hear the clock striking?"

"Why did they beat him? He had forgiven them. Then why did they hit him? Did it hurt him? Auntie, did it hurt?"

"Be quiet, I say, I am going to the dining room to have tea now."

"But perhaps it never happened, perhaps he was not beaten by them."

"I am going!"

"No, Auntie, don't go . . ." And again my madness took possession of me; I sobbed and sobbed, and began knocking my head against the wall."[3]

Young Tolstoy found it incomprehensible (and these memoirs are autobiographical) that Christ had been brutalized and his aunt was not interested enough to stay a little past tea time and talk about it. Nothing of value is ever preempted by trivia. When we allow a serious inquiry or challenge to pass unnoticed because we are in a hurry, we communicate that our faith is worth little.

To Listen

To make our witness effective, we must learn to distinguish between the flippant skeptic and the seeking skeptic. "God is dead!" has been said with two distinct intonations. Some years ago Thomas J. J. Altizer seemed to be saying it in the arrogant, academic flippancy of his fledgling professorship; maybe there was a discreet joy he harbored for ruffling the fur of the Bible Belt.

But there is another way to say that God is dead: It is the cry of honest but seeking skeptics. "God is dead, but I sincerely wish he were not." Hungering unbelief is capable of redemption. The weeping, seeking unbeliever is really a believer waiting for a studied compassion to tell him of Christ.

An effective defense will cause unbelievers to examine their position. But to say or imply, "You must not have thought about your position or you couldn't possibly believe that," is snobbery. Let us remember that while we are seeking to get people to examine Christianity for the first time, we will get much further if we don't ridicule or destroy their values—even if they seem unworthy to us. Listening is essential for compassion. Doubters must see us as listeners and not lecturers. Certain mechanical forms of witnessing cause us to emphasize schemes which obscure real reasoning. In the midst of some searching discussion, the impatient evangelist often takes a sidetrack to "The Four Spiritual Laws" or the "Roman Road to Salvation." This reversing of the cart and horse makes Christianity unwieldy for skeptics. They often abandon the conversation altogether.

We must be patient, and we must not be afraid to lose. Nobody likes a poor sport. The tendency of some zealots when backed into a corner by a good mind is to retreat behind pious clichés. The argument is not lost if the skeptic ends by saying, "I'll think about that!" But the discussion nearly always dies with no chance of resurrection after the pious clincher, "Just pray about it, dear brother, and trust God!" An effective defense reminds seekers that they must live with the consequences of their decisions.

The importance of discipline and understanding is paramount in this day of doubt. Salvation is a treasure, indeed. When it is so regarded, it will be spontaneously defended. As Christopher Morley said in *Kitty Foyle,* "Nobody knows what he really believes; you've got to guess at it by how you find yourself acting." When we find ourselves reacting to those who put us down for believing, we know we treasure our faith. But to defend what we believe, we must study.

When we have studied and are willing to risk ourselves, we will enter the marketplace of doubt and cry loudly, "I believe . . . and here's why!"

The greatest confession of the early church was the Caesarean confession of Simon, "Thou art the Christ, the Son of the Living God" (Matt 16:16).
Clyde E. Fant

Witness the man in the labour camp described by Solzhenitsyn, who had the bunk above his, and used to climb up into it in the evening, and take old, much-folded pieces of paper out of his pocket, and read them with evident satisfaction. It turned out that they had passages from the Gospels scribbled on them, which were his solace and joy in that terrible place. He would not, I feel sure, have been similarly comforted and edified by re-runs of old footage of religious T.V. programs.
Malcolm Muggeridge

Some men think the Earth is round, others think it flat; it is a matter capable of question. But if it is flat, will the King's command make it round? And if it is round, will the King's command flatten it?
Robert Bolt

6
The Facts
and
the Truth

A CHASM DIVIDES faith from science, religion from technology, worship from education and God from all academics. Faith takes one side of the road while science keeps to the other. The categories never come clearly labeled but in general we tend to speak of technical things as *facts* and spiritual things as *truth*.

But I am opposed to Don Quixote's assertion that facts are the enemy of truth. They really are fast friends. In fact, they are Siamese twins and the philosophical surgery which would separate them, would destroy them both. I know that Columbus discovered America. That is a fact but it is also the truth. It is both true and factual that the year was 1492. The ship was the Santa Maria: truth and fact.

Though in some ways the words *truth* and *fact* seem to be synonyms, they are remote synonyms. *Truth* is a warm word. *Fact* is a cold one. "Jenny, I love you truly," is, of course, warmer than "Jennifer, I love you factually." Truth is philosophical;

fact is empirical. Two plus two equals fact, but *truth* is too grand a word to use when we speak of common addition. Truth is elusive; fact is blatant. Truth is amorphous; fact, defined. Truth is prone to be quiet and reflective while fact is often loud. Truth is the fear of the astronaut; fact is the escape mechanism.

Here, perhaps, we move to the grand distinction that truth is mystical and fact is scientific. The creation is a miracle, both in fact and in truth. But the first Friday evening, as Adam and Eve went to bed, it was enough for truth to say, "The evening and the morning were the sixth day." But fact was full of unanswered questions. Breezes blew through Eden and truth loved the moving gentle air. Fact wanted to know the wind velocity. The sunlight fell in a splendor and truth enjoyed its warmth, but fact did not understand the riddle of helium. The animals of Eden were the peaceable kingdom, but fact sought only to understand their anatomy. The trees of the Garden were magnificent. They were the very kind of great trees truth would have carved hearts upon, but fact puzzled over photosynthesis.

They parted there in Eden, and truth went off to search for meaning while fact went to look for cave paintings. It was only a matter of time before truth would become the theologian and fact, the anthropologist.

"No, no, no," cry the wise. Truth and fact did argue in Eden. Head to head they debated foolishly. But when they looked down they always saw a common trunk and remembered that they were bound together. They have continued their foolish word games since.

But the twins have always had their worst problems when they considered biblical truth. It was hard for fact to admit that the basis of all science was born in the creativity of God. Usually when truth read Psalm 19, fact just shouted, "Hubble and Humason," at the top of his lungs. Their terms never came close either. Truth talked about eternity; fact about infinity. Truth liked meaning; fact wanted proof.

Many factualists cannot agree that there are any important facts to be found in the Bible. Using facts, they build locked systems of study which are logical and explainable. It is not that they hate biblical truth, but their insistence on fact prevents them from finding anything worthwhile at all in the miraculous Book of Truth.

These fact-lovers cannot understand how believers accept the truth so easily. They want to believe the truth, but facts come easier for them. They would like to live comfortably in a faith where fish swallow men and carpenters cure the crippled. But they cannot.

I must confess I am a truth-lover. It is as easy for me to accept Nebuchadnezzar's furnace as the one which warms my study. I accept the book of Jonah as I accept Marineland. But I know those who struggle to accept faith all of their lives and lose. For those who accept only fact and reject truth, their doubts are as costly as psychiatry.

Here and there those hooked on logic are confronted. "Why not just believe?" ask those who do. Perhaps because their intellect grows too proud to repent. Perhaps they fear the rejection of their peers who also love and live in the world of facts. Perhaps they refuse to believe because the world of truth seems alien to them. Perhaps they fear they will lose touch with the whole realm of reasonable science. If they should admit the existence of one angel, will not a multitude of heavenly hosts come and help them pack for their trip to the asylum?

Those who exclude all biblical truth disdain the whole idea of miracles. Most of them concede that if miracles could occur, they would hold great meaning. But they cannot bring themselves to believe.

A miracle is an event and like any other event has a reference point in time and space. A miracle may involve only one or two lives. Or, like the crossing of the Red Sea, it may concern thousands and have vast historical dimensions as well. History itself sometimes deals in the unexplainable. Whether or not I believe Washington crossed the Delaware does nothing to alter the reality of the event. Likewise, my acceptance or rejection of the Passover plague does not change its reality.

One may well ask, "If a miracle occurs in which none believe, does a miracle occur?" Disbelief cannot destroy a miracle but it may diminish its effect. The Israelites, seeing the Red Sea divided, would have been trapped and killed had they not believed in what they saw. The significance of the miracle lies not so much in God's dividing of the sea but in the safe passage of the Israelites through its midst. Salvation is the miracle's meaning; the dividing of the waters is the mechanical and less significant aspect of the event.

The resurrection is the central miracle of Scripture. But unbelieved, it loses its power. Paul could assert that "if Christ has not been raised, then . . . your faith is vain" (1 Cor 15:14). Without the miraculous resurrection, we perish hopelessly. But there is the identical result if the resurrection is true but unbelieved.

Those who love biblical truth see cold science as a great snare whose imprisonment in facts alone will not allow them to believe anything significant. The Bible is filled with historical facts, but these are often ignored by those who doubt precisely because these facts are woven into stories where miracles, ethics and history become hard to separate.

In the Bible miracles and teaching are woven inseparably together. The Ten Commandments come deeply embedded in a matrix of miracles: in cloven seas, mystic manna and fiery shrubs. The Beatitudes are beautiful, but they come packaged in stories of healed children, cleansed lepers, and men who walk on the seas.

Further, the great Bible teachings of salvation are born in two great miracles. The Old Testament gathers itself about God's redemption from bondage. The New focuses on salvation from sin. Tamper with the Red Sea and you alter the teaching of Old Testament redemption. Tamper with the resurrection and you alter New Testament salvation. Faith grows from the event.

Here we see the difference between the facts and the truth. Science cannot be separated from a predictability in nature and retain integrity. Genetics cannot set aside Mendel's laws even for a moment and expect the system to hold together. Chemistry may not give up its confidence in molecular compounding, or there is no key. But biblical truth derives its great meaning from events that break with science. We know the physical behavior of water. Yet water misbehaves at the Red Sea. The resurrection is a physiological impossibility. Dead men do not live again, but one man did and Christianity was born.

God created his universe in a predictable way. All of the phenomena on which we are so dependent always come in an expected way. Sunrise, rain, gravity, oxygen, the lymphatic system, DNA molecules, transistor flow—great sciences are built on God's predictability. Great faith is built upon God's ability to cut across his predictable systems. When that happens, miracles occur. To be sure, it does not happen often, making science possible. But it does happen sometimes, making faith.

The National Aeronautics and Space Administration depends on God's predictability to remain in existence. All the sciences use his predictability to culture buttermilk, ignite Bunsens, feather props, brake locomotives, run hatcheries and analyze the monotonous computer codes of space probes.

We have fortunately moved beyond the place where the alchemists and theologians of the Middle Ages viewed nature as God's armor and weaponry to contend with us. Hurricanes, earthquakes and typhoons were once thought to be the thunderbolts of Jehovah. When he wearied with a nation, he merely laid a bacteria of some sort on a nameless plate, and sat back to watch the plague decimate his world, which so justly deserved it.

From such a preposterous view of nature, scientists who drained swamps or put up lightning rods were seen as adversaries of God. After all, if God wishes to strike a rebellious church with lightning, should he be thwarted by a lightning rod from doing his will? Should Galveston build a sea wall if God wishes to flog the city with hurricanes? By such thinking the Corps of Engineers becomes an army of anti-God militants thwarting God's eternal purposes with flood control.

Perhaps in our day, quarrels over abortion, birth control and, certainly, evolution often stem from this fact-versus-truth debate. Evolutionists have a way of arrogantly sneering at creationists. Some Christians often stoop to cheap tricks instead of real arguments. Sometimes orthodoxy gets cute to avoid the necessity of sound argument. In *Inherit the Wind,* Brady cried against the geologists that he was more interested in the Rock of Ages than he was the age of rocks.

It has been hard for Christians in our day to find out exactly what they believe because within Christianity there is a great division about the nature of miracles. Many churchgoers no longer consider them to be true. When theologians argue, who can be trusted? Those who deny miracles have interpreted hell to be the "fiery, swelling ignorance" of the Bible Belt. Some fundamentalists believe it to be directly beneath the basement floor of ivy-league divinity schools!

Technology did not set out to redefine miracles. It just continued doing impressive and unbelievable things, so that the unusual became the ordinary. Moses created a wall of water at the Red Sea. So did the Corps of Engineers at Hoover Dam. Paratroopers prove how easy it is to leap from the pinnacle of any temple and land unhurt. Jesus once walked on water. Now we have the Cypress Garden Water Show. Both Elijah and the Wright Brothers flew.

There is no real conflict between technology and miracle, but we are not so easily awed today. One often imagines how General Washington would react if he could be taken from his day and dropped in the middle of ours. The shock would likely overwhelm him. We have exactly the reverse problem. Technology underwhelms us. We have gotten used to bread that browns itself, houses that regulate their own temperature and ships that orbit the planet in a mere ninety minutes. General Washington would have been struck dumb by the window-box full of little people that we call television. When too many unbelievable things are happening, everything becomes believable. Jenner's vaccine saved more people from disease in a month than Jesus did in his entire life. Jenner's vaccine is considered good science, but not miraculous.

But technology unintentionally did something worse than diminish miracles. Like an egotistic Roman emperor, it proclaimed its own deity. Technology became at once the grand savior and the great enslaver. McLuhan's Global Village was not without an altar. Technology was the totem, and it demanded worship.

McLuhan's idol was a high-tech god whose electronic giggle was set off by the plunger of the toaster. This god taught us to pray, "Give us this day, our daily toast." It cried out behind the towrope of the power launch as it strapped on its skis, "Lord, if it be you, bid me come to you on the water." It spoke from Sesame Street and said, "Let the little children come unto me and forbid them not." It said from every computer reel, "Why keep all these things and ponder them in your heart? Give them to a soft-disc system." It cried its technological atonement from the Red Cross Bloodmobile, "Without the shedding of blood, you have no life—AB or O positive!"

It is hard not to worship a superb technology crammed with miracles. A miraculous technology seems to lord it over a miraculous God. For technology made no demands on our morality. One cannot have the miracle of new birth without submission to the domination of Jesus Christ as Lord. But one could have the miracle of birth control, and repudiate both God and technology. More and more as the great transistorized, stainless steel totem became adored, its machines stalked the earth, subject only to the cyborgs who created them and doctored them when they got sick.

The psychological revolution which accompanied the rise of technology abandoned the biblical definitions of man. We were forced to find our identity in the dialog of psychologists who seemed rarely to agree on how we could locate the shortest route to meaning. Removing sin was a matter of conditioning or adjustment. "I'm OK—You're OK" is a new way of viewing our depravity and living with it. Skinnerians overlooked the protest of ethics and dealt with setting us free of all moral requirements. Psychological technology was, however, generally hard put. For most, traditional psychiatry seemed an endless therapy that never healed. Innovative psychiatry, on the other hand, was spastic and experimental.

Technology had its greatest psychological impact in the creation of altered states. Uppers and downers, legally or illegally dispensed, were creating fields of moods. But psychology itself, like other sciences, has not fulfilled its promises.

Pure science can have no other end for it pursues facts alone, and the great issues of meaning lie always with truth. We cannot castigate those who follow facts and create a magnificent world of technological miracle—they often make life easier and safer. But we can say to them, "You have not gone far enough. Come with us to Christ who is the epicenter of meaning and who once told the world he was the very truth of God."

We have painted ourselves into a corner and have become victims of the scientific monster that we have created.
Vance Havner

Philosophy and science have not always been friendly toward the idea of God, the reason being that they are dedicated to the task of accounting for things and are impatient with anything that refuses to give an account of itself.
A. W. Tozer

Could he have created anything he wanted to?
Of course. He's God.
Do you like what he created?
Yes. Yes, I do.
Battlefields and slums and insane asylums?
Well, he didn't create those.
Who did?
We did.
Who's we? I didn't create them.
Mankind did. And you're part of mankind and so am I.
But God created mankind?
Yes.
Why did he create mankind if mankind was going to create battlefields and insane asylums and slums?
Madeleine L'Engle

7
Meaning in Miracles

WE ARE THE children of Adam.

Our interest in science and learning is no accident. Our very name, *Homo sapiens,* means "knower." Our five senses have allowed us to gather and classify all phenomena: this surface is smooth and that is rough. This tastes sweet; that is acrid. She is lovely; he is homely. Listen to the viola and evensong. Quit banging on the pipes! Thus we move through life sampling and categorizing existence.

But we learn more easily than we trust. We are forever sticking our index finger on the white surfaces beneath "Wet Paint" signs. We will not believe without a sample of cool pigment on our finger. If our finger comes up dry, we will lay our hand on the wall, and if necessary push and rub the defiant surface to make it yield a smudge.

Touching wet walls is the Adam in us. We are incurable believers, yet paradoxically incurable unbelievers. Adam had only one "Wet Paint" sign in Eden. The sign clearly said "Bad

Apples!" Adam must have leaned back against the sign for days fondling the fruit and asking himself, "Is it or not?"

Adam was created to live forever. He wondered just how long a man could live without testing the truth of the sign. The fever to know raged. Had the Lord God posted the sign only to drive him mad with the lust to know? Desire welled up and consumed him. Satan tempted Adam with the taunt that there was yet one thing he didn't know—the tactile feel of the forbidden, the sensuous delight of paint on the finger.

Adam may have led us into doubt but he has not kept us there. We gather data for ourselves beneath the signs of our existence. Some of us doubt all and are called atheists. Some of us doubt most and are called agnostics. Some of us doubt little and are called believers.

UFOs

What exactly does it mean to be a believer? It means that the original hunger of Adam—the drive to know by experience— has been abridged. Believers can lay aside their need to prove the paint is wet. They have said to those rubbing the walls that they are willing to trust the sign. Miracles lie at the point of faith where we are unable to gather data. We are liberated to believe what is beyond our understanding.

Some years ago, UFO reports were coming in rather quickly. Flying saucers were landing here and there, all across the country, alarming observers—which seemed to me their only real function. One report came in which particularly angered me as an unbeliever in UFOs: a man in my hometown saw a flying saucer at a prominent intersection. He was visibly shaken, telling local police he had seen a saucer-shaped craft flying over Omaha.

My wife read me the newspaper item on this poor hysterical man who had to be taken to a local hospital. "What do you think he saw?" my wife asked.

"Nothing," I said with a great deal of irritation. "Have you noticed how everybody sees UFOs but no one ever takes a picture? Do you know why nobody takes a picture?"

My wife could see I was becoming hot. "No," she said simply. "Do you know why?"

"Because it's hard to photograph schizophrenia," I said in anger.

A few days later just at dusk we were going to the market only a block from our home. As we came to a stop sign I saw these little saucer-shaped blips of light circulating in the sky. I studied the sky and said to my wife, "Oh, look. What are those things?"

"Do you know what they look like?" she asked. We both knew what they looked like. I squinted as she drily asked, "OK, where's your camera?"

There clearly was something there; it was the interpretation of the phenomena that was the problem. In this instance my own viewpoint was clouded by unbelief. Once I had stamped my foot on the floor and said there were no flying saucers, only intellectual repentance could make change possible. But that has never been easy.

Saul once smirked over superstitious Christians who believed in the resurrection. He no doubt thanked God that he had been to the Jewish seminary and recognized primitive religion when he saw it. Then all of a sudden he was confronted by a desert specter and found himself asking, "Who is it?" Had my wife been there she would have said, "OK, seminary grad, where's your camera?" Paul had to deal with a phenomenon he had already decided not to believe in. When the Christ of the Damascus Road said, "I am Jesus of Nazareth," Paul did not have the audacity to say, "But you're in the graveyard; I've been telling everyone about it."

In other world religions, miracles and legends may be non-existent or nonessential to faith. Not so with Christianity. Christ's birth was miraculous as was his resurrection. If we try to take away Christianity's miraculous heart, we destroy it.

Suspending Nature

Biblical miracles "set aside" nature for the welfare of people. This shows how much we mean to God.

Nature can be kind. When it is, we see God in the seagull's nest and the mountain stream. But what about when nature is not kind? What conclusions do we draw when quakes rip cities or villages are decimated with the plague? Do we say God is a fiend who cares nothing for us?

Nature alone was not the way for God to say, "Man has a special meaning to me." But by suspending nature God could demonstrate that we mean more to him than the created order.

Jesus ended Bartimaeus's blindness, and gave him sight by a supernatural act. The miracle proved that Bartimaeus was important to God. Jesus fed the five thousand because he had compassion on the hungry crowd. In considering such supernatural events we see our cosmic importance. Without a God who gets involved in the natural world we are but unimportant microbes.

André Malraux has said, "The greatest mystery is not that we have been flung at random among the profusion of the earth and the galaxy of the stars, but that in this prison we can fashion images of ourselves sufficiently powerful to deny our nothingness."[1] But he is only partly right. We would be nothing if we were not loved by God.

When we were children, the monsters of the dark seemed real and fanged, lurking in the hallway just outside our door. We heard thunderous footfalls in the gloom. But they turned out to be only our father who heard us crying and came to comfort us. We never saw him in the darkness, but we felt his touch and knew he was there. The universe is vast and sometimes dark, but we are not alone.

Decoding Miracles

Still the very miracle in which God declares his promise always needs interpretation. Is it our Father's hand in the darkness, or did we imagine that he touched us? Did he really speak or was it but the howling of the gales? And even if we conclude that he did speak, what did he mean?

Sometimes decoding a miracle can be tough. Conservative Christians do not doubt Christ's first public miracle. But interpreting it is painful for some of them. They wish the whole thing was reversed, that Jesus had changed several crocks of wine into sweet, pure water.

Jesus' cursing of the fig tree for its lack of fruit is difficult to decipher as well. It is perhaps his most ambiguous miracle. It forces us to trust without understanding. While I do not doubt the truth of it, it seems to lack the relevance of a healing.

Decoding can also involve distinguishing between a miracle and a trick. To the trick we say, "How did you do that?" To the miracle, we bow our heads and say, "I believe!" Moses was enchanted with the superiority of Jehovah of Sinai over Ra of Thebes. Jehovah had made Moses a miracle worker, a cobra-maker first-class. By the power of *Yahweh,* Moses could make a snake. Meanwhile, back in Thebes, the court magicians were learning how to throw down sticks and make snakes. One day they met, stick to stick, cobra to cobra, trick to miracle.

For a moment it looked as though the magicians were miracle workers, themselves. But they were only tricksters. What did Moses learn that day in court, after his cobra had become a fat, dumb cane again, gorged with Egyptian serpents? After the Red Sea he probably realized that cobra-making was frivolous compared to nation-saving. Pharaoh clapped for the writhing serpent, but he put ashes on his head and wept when the Passover angel slew his son.

The Freedom of God

Human significance lay behind the whole Passover miracle, and all the miracles of the exodus. It wasn't Moses who said, "Let my people go!" It was God. God acted in the interest of human freedom, for he himself is free. He cannot be imprisoned in the natural world.

Chesterton is right when he says that a universe with no possibility of miracles imprisons God in the system. "A miracle only means the liberty of God. The Catholic Church believed that man and God both had a sort of spiritual freedom. Calvinism took away the freedom from man, but left it to God. Scientific materialism binds the Creator Himself; it chains up God as the Apocalypse chained the devil. It leaves nothing free in the universe."[2] Deists captured God by allowing him to create the universe but not be involved in it. God was extraordinary, they said, but he no longer did anything extraordinary.

When I have asked liberal thinkers why they reject the supernatural birth of Christ, they often reply that if he were fully human, he must have had an ordinary birth. The argument sounds good, unless you press the corollary that he must also have an ordinary death. To be fully human, Jesus must remain dead since that is a customary human condition. Such an ordinary Christ is so human he gets lost in the crowd of poetic mystics who start religions and pass away.

In denying God the power to resurrect Christ, they deny God the freedom to live above nature and beyond reason. Surely our tiny thinking is a narrow cell for a cosmic God. Believing in miracles sets God free to work in any way he wishes.

God's freedom can at times seem harsh. God set Israel free

by killing the first-born of all of Egypt. Indeed the whole Egyptian cavalry was lost in the Red Sea. At Jericho many Canaanites died when the walls collapsed. God loved the children of Jericho, but for his own infinite reasons, some perished while others lived. If God does not appear gracious to all, we must remember that he acts for reasons that cannot always be seen without the perspectives of time and destiny.

If God is free he can go any direction he wishes to accomplish his ends. He may either tamper with the tastebuds of the wedding guests so they think the water is wine, or he may in fact change well-water to port. When the prophet is hungry the ravens bring him food. He could just as easily have multiplied his last loaf of bread indefinitely. When the mob is hungry, he may multiply the bread or he may as easily send a flock of ravens to bring food.

So often miracles tend to get confused with coincidence. When the Israelites were dying of hunger someone likely said, "The quails just happened to be flying over Sinai. It's our lucky day!" Perhaps when they sat down to dinner that night, someone else remarked how fortunate they were to be in the flyway of a million quail. Someone else may have been just as convinced that God specially acted to send the birds.

No doubt some who traveled with Moses in Sinai never saw either God's miracles or his freedom. Remember manna was only a miracle for a while. After a week of manna most of them were saying, "Good grief, not again!" Probably some of the five thousand, even while their mouths were filled with fish and bread, wished Jesus had provided figs and cheese.

The Bible contains from first to last the tale of God's miraculous acts in human history. Each time God acted he said that we have special meaning to him. With every miracle we gained a new quality of life that taught us how special we are. The Lord of the universe is our special, redeeming friend.

*Dostoevsky's novels bore the mark of his experience
with the Tsarist police. He never forgot how he was led
to the place of execution, to be left standing
for what seemed hours, before he was told that his
death sentence had been commuted to exile.*
Niels C. Nielson, Jr.

*For what do I wish to say, O Lord my God,
but that I know not whence I came neither into this
life-in-death. Or should I call it death-in-life? And yet
the consolations of thy mercy have sustained me from
the very beginning, as I have heard from my fleshly parents,
from whom and in whom thou didst form me in time
—for I cannot myself remember.*
Augustine

*Tomorrow we shall meet,
Death and I—
And he shall thrust his sword
Into one who is wide awake.*
Dag Hammarskjöld

8
The
Miracle
of Life

STILL FORMED IN terra-cotta clay Adam once waited for the Lord God to breathe into him the wonderful breath of life. After receiving the breath of the Creator, Adam stood and stretched, magnificently alive. For Adam the word *life* did not exist since the word *death* was unknown. Such words always come in pairs. In the wake of sin Adam learned the whole truth. We, like Adam, in the passing of years, must come to grips with one great inevitability: death. George Bernard Shaw once remarked that death is the ultimate statistic—it affects one out of one. Death becomes a mockery of life.

Since death is so final, most of us do all we can to avoid it. Unconsciously we act in self-preservation. We keep to our side of the white line on the freeway. We strap ourselves in roller coasters. We stop, look and listen at railroad crossings. Life is dear and precautions are regular. Considering this, salvation is the most reasonable step one can take toward ultimate life, eternal self-preservation.

Eternal life is the gift of God. He alone holds the power to make the dead live again. In the New Testament there are at least thirty-five separate references to the resurrection of Christ. Most are passive. They read like this:

Acts 2:24—God raised him up . . .

Acts 2:32—This Jesus God raised up . . .

Acts 3:15—whom God raised from the dead . . .

Acts 3:26—God, having raised up his servant, . . .

The meaning of expressing the event in the passive voice is immense. Jesus put absolute and utter faith in God. If Christ's Father had not raised him to life, he would still be dead and Matthew Arnold's awful words in *Obermann Once More* would be true:

Far hence he lies in the lorn Syrian town,

And on his grave with shining eyes,

The Syrian stars look down.

But his death was not permanent! As his Father once created human life, he now created Easter life, and death was defeated.

Jesus and the Resurrection

Most of the ancient religions had deities that came in pairs: Isis had Serapis; Baal had Ashtaroth; and Zeus had Hera. The New Testament word for "resurrection" is *anastasis*. In the literature of the New Testament this beautiful word becomes the consort of Christ.

Most of the pagan gods and goddesses were sexual divinities. Their worship glorified their fertility. Baal loved Ashtaroth and their celestial affair produced an abundance of spring crops. Their fertility was symbolized in cultic rites of prostitution. In Roman mythology, the lusty, leathery Pluto ravished Proserpina. The birth of life in the animal and plant world was the result of the sexuality of these heroes of Olympus.

But with Jesus and *anastasia* there was a different definition of love. In the resurrected Christ life was on a higher plateau than deified sexuality. Sex can be brutal as in a rape. Sex can be perverted. It can be disappointing as when barrenness leaves couples childless. And of course, sex, like all other aspects of human physiology, is slain by death, never to rise again. But resurrection life never brutalized. It was never perverted. Death cannot intimidate this marvelous Easter life. Jesus and *anastasia* were the conquering couple for whom the world so long had waited.

There is no English word that really translates *anastasis*. The most elementary meaning of the word is to "stand again!" But Jesus, the risen one, was not merely a resuscitated redeemer, standing again with a restored physiology. The post-Easter Christ did not merely wake from decay. His life was rather a passing into a kind of superlife.

What was the new life that Christ introduced to the world really like? Substance that allowed him to eat fish (Lk 24:42) but also vanish (Lk 24:31). He was physical enough to have scars (Jn 20:27), but so ethereal that he went up in a cloud out of sight (Acts 1:9). He was so substantial that he could cook breakfast by the sea (Jn 21:9), but so lacking in physical density that he could enter a room that had every door locked (Jn 20:19). After the brutality of crucifixion, the resurrection shouted out the glorious immutability of Christ.

Jesus demonstrated that this superlife keeps two things straight. First, resurrection is not merely spiritual; the body is involved. Second, it is not merely a bodily proposition. A dead body come alive again is at worst a zombie and at best a resuscitation.

During Jesus' own life, he resurrected other people from the dead. But it is really not accurate to use the word *resurrection* with Lazarus or the widow's son in Nain. For while there was clearly no question that they were dead and restored to life, they were as dependent on pulse, nutrition and respiration as they had ever been. Not so with Christ! Further, the widow's son at Nain and Lazarus himself had to go through the ordeal of dying all over again.

Our Resurrection

The victory of real resurrection is that it will not permit decay. The Bible states that the resurrection of all believers will be much like Jesus' own. While he laid in the grave for only three days, many others have been dead for centuries. But time is inconsequential. St. Francis, dead by over seven centuries, will one day be as perfectly alive as Dwight L. Moody, Simon Peter or Jesus himself.

The nature of resurrection was taken far more seriously by ancient Christians than it is by modern ones. The Corinthians in Paul's day wanted to know what would happen to the dead of their congregation at the coming of the Lord (see 1 Cor 15:51-58). The primitive Christian community ran into the Roman practice of cremation and despised it for its blatant antiresurrection character. Cremation seemed to early Christians to complicate matters. Therefore the catacombs became immense burial grounds awaiting resurrection. Those bodies were partly devoured by beasts, sometimes charred with flame, sometimes mauled by gladiators. Still, Christians believed God would one day reclaim the bodies of all those who had died in Christ.

These early Christians were not the last ones to think of resurrection so materially. Bertrand Russell, in a *reductio ad absurdum* argument, posed the problem of cannibal cultures. He considered cannibals who had derived most of their nutrition by feeding on other human bodies. What a tangled problem this would be on resurrection day when God began trying to reconstitute those whose bodies actually owed their own substance to the other human bodies which had nourished them!

Resurrection, however, must not be thought of in purely physiological terms. What, for instance, is the quantitative difference between a man dead five minutes and the man he had been five minutes before? He has no life. His tissues are the same, and still so alive that someone else may benefit from them. His kidneys can purify blood for another. His corneas may make other sightless eyes see.

One of the shortcomings of science is that its ignorance of resurrection life has led it to deify biological life. Some scientists are heady about their ability to extend or even create life. But the life in a controlled laboratory environment can never approach Easter life. Easter life not only survives; it transcends every other kind of life.

Objections Raised

Skeptics cry against all possibility of resurrection. They raise any number of "proofs" to silence all that the Bible claims. For instance, there is the so-called Swoon Theory. This says that Jesus never came alive again because he never really died. He merely fainted from the trauma of crucifixion, and everybody thought he was dead. However, the cool, damp, moist interior of the tomb revived him. He walked out of the tomb and people believed he had come back to life. This view implies that he really did die later, after the resurrection "myth" became established.

There is also the Wrong Tomb Theory which suggests that the women in their grief and confusion went to the wrong sepulcher, that first Easter morning. Not finding Jesus' body they assumed he was living again. Had they been more careful in locating the proper tomb, the world would have been spared the confusion their erroneous announcement caused. It was an innocent mistake, say theorists; the women were not to blame since they were from Galilee and unacquainted with the cemeteries of Jerusalem.

Another theologian has devised the Christ of Faith, one who is not the eternal Christ sent by God. The Christ of Faith is one manufactured by devoted followers who loved Jesus so much they were blind to his humanity. They innocently exaggerated his miraculous deeds. After his death, deluded by their great love for him, they credited him with resurrection. Such reasoning is a return to the chicken-and-egg question. Does faith create miracles or miracles, faith? The Christ-of-Faith concept would teach that Jesus' resurrection did not create their belief, but their belief created his resurrection.

There are many other theories that try to explain the resurrection in purely natural terms. One hybrid theory uses both spiritual and material explanations. The view, popularized by Leslie Weatherhead, is based on hypnosis. Weatherhead points out that good hypnotists can influence people to such a degree that they feel unreal stimuli as though they were real. Hypnotists can tell their subjects, for instance, that a pencil is a white-hot poker. On being touched by a pencil the physical symptoms of a burn will appear. Christ, said Dr. Weatherhead, was able with his great mind to hypnotize himself into believing that the tomb was a great oven that instantly vaporized his body.

While this explanation is too outlandish to take seriously, I am grateful to Weatherhead for one piece in his logic which points out the difference between hallucination and apparition. If only one person sees a dead man alive again, it may be said to be a hallucination. If more than one sees it, it may be termed an apparition. Most of the resurrection appearances of Christ were witnessed by several people at a time. On one occasion as many as five hundred people at once saw Christ alive again (1 Cor 15:6).

This, then, lends credibility to the Bible account. Many apologists have argued for the historicity of the resurrection with the same line of thinking. They often point out that most of the apostles were martyred rather than say that the resurrection had not occurred. Paul Little, for example, wrote: "Men will die for what they *believe* to be true, though it may actually be false. They do not, however, die for what they *know* is a lie."[1]

Little is saying that the martyrdom of the disciples is witness to the resurrection. Indeed the Greek word *martys* means "witness." The strongest way that we may bear our witness is to die in declaring it.

In addition, the diverse elements of the story lend credibility to it. The gospel writers are careful to record the first doubts of the witnesses themselves concerning the resurrection. The pandemonium that resulted that first Easter morning is jumbled. The very disorder in the narration suggests the truth of the event. If the church had been concocting a myth, it would have done it much more smoothly. The resurrection stories are the most tangled episodes of the gospels.

At first report they all were skeptical. Mark's gospel says of all the apostles: "Now when he rose early on the first day of the week, he appeared first to Mary Magdalene. . . . She went out and told those who had been with him. . . . But . . . they would not believe it. After this he appeared in another form to two of them, as they were walking in the country. And they went back and told the rest, but they did not believe them" (Mk 16:9-13). Luke recorded that their "words seemed to them an idle tale" (Lk 24:11). Thomas's skepticism was obnoxious (Jn 20:25). The church had to be convinced. Jesus stayed around for almost six weeks showing them by many infallible proofs that he was indeed resurrected. Then they went out to tell the impossible story to the world.

They did it with all of the credibility they could muster, but to many it sounded like a hoax. Still they all knew it was the chief of miracles. Paul listed it so high in importance in his letter to the Romans that he said without believing in it, there could be no salvation (Rom 10:9). If there was no resurrection life, there was nothing saving in any of Christ's promises (1 Cor 15:14).

The resurrection is the one great authenticating miracle of the Bible. It is the life miracle, the last reply to the Carpentarians' reason. Absurdity has been thrown into the abyss. We may look into the womb of the universe and see that the cosmos is not barren, the universe is not absurd. Life is not an empty cry from the abyss. Life is not biology alone. Life is eternal. Beyond the path of reason is the mystery of life unending. Christ destroyed death. Impermanence is gone. Eternity rises in rich hope. We live in Christ—and forever!

Who can take away suffering without entering it? . . .
No God can save us except a suffering God.
Henri Nouwen

Healing and the healing of the whole man are creative acts
of God, no matter what the agent may be.
John Sutherland Bonnell

One that heals with the Holy Word . . . will best drive
away sickness from the body of the faithful.
Zend-Avesta

9
Christt the Healer

THE THIRTY-FIVE miracles of Jesus which are specifically described in Scripture fall into four categories. Nine times Jesus countermanded the natural world. For instance, he turned the water into wine (Jn 2:1-11), stilled the storm (Mt 8:23-27) and fed the multitude (Mt 14:13-21). Six of his recorded miracles were exorcisms (for example, Mk 1:21-28; Mt 12:22; Lk 8:26-39). Three times he raised the dead (Mt 9:18-26; Lk 7:11-15; Jn 11:1-44). But the bulk of his miraculous acts were devoted to the suffering. Seventeen times he healed. Jesus had every right to the title of Great Physician.

Pain is a prison. It is the enemy of all communion. It alienates us from the conversation and commerce of the day. When pain grows, we wait in a bubble of isolation for the fiery screams of our nervous systems to pass. When pain is severe enough, we may actually pray to die.

Maria was a woman full of bounce, a lover of people, enraptured by the conversation she could not only manage but stimulate. Enter pain and carcinoma. Enter isolation. The last I saw her, she wailed in agony in ward thirty-two, a dehumanized sallow-eyed and sunken-cheeked replica of life. She and her cancer died the same afternoon. At the moment of her passing, she abandoned life without even speaking to her friends. Indeed, she did not even want them present.

A miracle of healing enters that strange world of 98.6-degree dark interiors. Here beneath the surface of our personalities there lies a strange cosmos of gristle and pulsating tendons, of ventricles and spongy glands, of rubbery pipes and cartilage. When the healing occurs, God enters the dark world: the amino acids stand to attention, nuclei bow in preparation for the coming storm of renovation and the miracle passes through the dark warm world of human life.

Disease always cringed before the healing miracle of Christ. Consider the woman with the incessant hemorrhage (Lk 8:43-48). She grew old hoping for a cure, coping with life. When she had contracted the condition, Jesus was still only a teen-ager. She craved wholeness. She spent all she had searching for health. Finally, she heard of Jesus. She came to him. She touched his garment and instantly was healed. We do not know what caused her bleeding, but let us say it was leukemia. This is a poor guess, but if it were leukemia let us observe what happened. The quarreling corpuscles in her arteries and veins ceased their disputes. The white cells gave up their ghastly civil struggle with their red brothers. Instantly the cellular cannibalism ended, and she was well.

Perhaps you object that such a description of the miracle is too clinical. But let us remember that if the poor woman was to be free of leukemia, the deadly interaction of her blood cells had to be reversed. If we cannot believe such things happened, we cannot believe this miracle was possible.

Jesus' healing miracles correct nature gone malevolent. His

nature miracles do too. Jesus once rebuked the storm. He spoke to the wind: moving molecules of hydrogen, oxygen, carbon dioxide and nitrogen. He rebuked the storm, and at his rebuke the wind subsided. But how did Christ communicate to the molecules? They have no auditory nerves to hear. They are merely kinetic. Still, at his rebuke the molecules did in some way yield. The wild atmosphere was tamed. The scientific mechanics of healing and stilling storms are complex.

When I was a boy in Oklahoma, a faith healer came to our small town and created a stir of controversy with his crusades. One of those who came forward for healing was a small blind woman who ran a rehabilitation concession in the city post office. The healer told the woman that she could be cured if she would send her guide dog home. She could not bring herself to release her hold of the harness. She remained blind when the faith healer left. In time, he became one of the popular faith healers of our day. The reaction of our hometown to the healer was much like the reaction of Nazarenes to Jesus. It was said of the city, that Christ could "do no mighty works there. . . . And he marveled because of their unbelief" (Mk 6:5).

Faith is important for healing. Let us ask three questions concerning Christ's healing miracles. How did Christ heal? When did he do it? Why did he heal?

How Did Christ Heal?

How? Sometimes he used saliva, sometimes touch. Sometimes he embraced the sufferer. Sometimes he spoke to the disease. Sometimes he forgave sin, and the cure came with his forgiveness.

When we look at how Jesus healed, the word that strikes us is *immediately*. Twenty-three times in the New Testament the word is used to tell how Jesus healed or performed other miracles. In every one of the seventeen recorded healing miracles, it was immediately clear to those at hand that the suffering one had been healed.

I once heard a faith healer with a most unusual approach. He would stand before a large crowd and say, "There is a man in this audience who is on row thirty, and he has been suffering for years from kidney infections. Sir, God wants you to know that you have been miraculously healed! Stand and give God the glory!" And then, in a kind of response to the healer's clairvoyance, the man would stand on what appeared to be row thirty and give God the glory. And in a similarly clairvoyant method, patients with heart disease, ulcers, colitis, rheumatism and so on were cured row by row, section by section. But it was not anything that anybody could see.

I was skeptical, because I remembered a family who called me after a faith-healing service to tell me that their diabetic daughter would never again need insulin. "The Lord has miraculously healed her," they said. They confidently reported that they had the word of their evangelist. Their daughter was cured! I rejoiced with them, but reminded them that they should watch for early signs of insulin shock.

To demonstrate their faith, they threw away their store of insulin and syringes. A week later they called me in the small hours of the morning to report that their daughter was in a deep coma and could not be roused. I encouraged them to take her to the emergency room of the nearest hospital. Only the skill of a physician was able to deliver their daughter from the "miracle" of the faith healer. Jesus' miracles were instantaneous and apparent. He gave false hopes to none.

How did he heal? He did so without personal gratuities or love offerings. In the last decade one of America's faith healers confessed before her death that she had amassed a fortune through her crusades. At the time of her death, she had jewels and antiques worth over a million dollars purchased from the love offerings of her devotees. There was no hint of selfishness or personal gain in Jesus' ministry among the poor of Palestine. Every disciple should glory in following a Christ who died in poverty.

When Did Christ Heal?

When did Jesus heal? Whenever people asked for it. In cases of demoniacs or the dumb who could not ask, Jesus set them free anyway (Mt 9:32; 12:22; 17:14). The great concern of those who brought their mute friends to Christ stirred him to touch and heal those who could not ask for their own healing.

As we said earlier of miracles in general, Christ usually healed in response to human desperation. Catherine Marshall in *A Man Called Peter* tells how she was healed during a broadcast as her husband Peter Marshall preached on the healing power of Christ.

The wife of a good pastor friend of mine was hopelessly stricken with cancer. During exploratory surgery it was diagnosed as "terminal within a few weeks." She sensed her own desperation and yielded in total obedience to Christ's will, and she was granted healing. Every time I see her now, years later, I am reminded what God can do with desperation.

Let us not forget that salvation always comes when the lost are made aware of their utter helplessness. Why should the same thing not be true in physiology? If God can cure desperate souls, why not desperate bodies? The woman of Luke 8 was cured partly because she had tried everything else to no avail. Bartimaeus of Jericho cried out, soul-weary with his blindness. Those near him rebuked him and told him to be silent. He refused. He wanted to see—he was desperate to behold the light of day. And he did.

There are times when Jesus asks a blind man—perhaps a beggar—"What wilt thou have me do?" The answer should have been obvious, and yet he asks. He wants the one in need to deal with his own priorities. Does he really want to be well? Hypochondria is a formidable barrier to health. Unlike Bartimaeus, hypochondriacs know no desperation to be well— only a furious hunger to be pitied.

For years a hypochondriac was a member of my church. On pastoral calls, I often stopped by her home. Whenever she served me tea, the tea cart would be crowded with medicines. Often, as I observed her taking two or three pills during a single cup of tea, an overwhelming sense of anger arose within me. Like Christ in the Temple, I wanted to turn over the trays of drugs and drive out the demons of hypochondria which filled her with self-pity. She never asked me to pray for her to get well. She reveled in her supposed illnesses. Jesus usually healed when those who asked demonstrated a genuine feeling of desperation.

At the point of desperation physiology and spirituality have the most in common. Repentance is not a drab recounting of error. Repentance is utter desperation: engulfed in our own sin, we are utterly overwhelmed at our powerlessness to rise above it. Repentance is facing the fact that our sins resulted in the cross. We cry to God, "Lord, have mercy on me a sinner."

Likewise, Jesus heals when we cry, "Lord, have mercy!" There are times when the desperation of suffering drives us to the wall of consciousness. Antibiotics and chemotherapy have all failed, and the specialists say, "I'm sorry, there's nothing more we can do." The gallant Christ then looms in compassion above our desperation.

Why Did Christ Heal?

Perhaps the most difficult question of Christ's miracles of healing is why. Why did he heal when he came primarily to redeem?

I don't believe he worked his miracles to confirm his Messiah-ship. Yet neither were they incidental to his greater purpose. The answer must lie in his godhood. He healed primarily because he was a Christ of love. Five times prior to a miracle the Scriptures say, "He was moved with compassion." Eight times prior to a miracle, "He had compassion on them."

Perhaps the why of Christ's healing should not be so puzzling. Would you expect the Messiah to walk by a crippled child and say, "Poor thing! I could help you run in the sunlight in complete health, but what good would it do? You would only grow old in fifty years and die anyway. And after all, I am on a mission of salvation. Believe you me, little girl, temporal suffering is just nothing compared to what awaits"? A Christ who was *that* busy with saving would not be loving enough to redeem.

Still, he was not *primarily* the Great Physician but the savior of the world. Had he been only a healer, he could have stood on Olivet and rebuked all suffering at once. He came to earth to die. Yet the same love that brought him here to die caused him to heal while he awaited his cross. In anticipation of the iron ripping through his own wrists, he could not be flippant about the pain he saw destroying others.

Jesus also performed the nature miracles to deal with other kinds of suffering. The fear of his apostles when they were caught in a violent storm made him come to them on the sea. His compassion for the hungry among the peasants made him divide the loaves. His compassion for the embarrassed wedding host prompted him to turn water into wine.

Relieving discomfort, however, was not his only aim. As I said earlier, suffering destroys all interest in other values, either social or spiritual. So by restoring health, Christ eased the way for those who were in pain to become interested in eternal matters.

One final suggestion may be made as to why Jesus healed. He viewed the human body as a temple. Jesus' indictment as a false Messiah arose from outrage at his statement, "Destroy this temple and I will build it again in three days." The body was the temple. A healthy temple is a better center of worship than a diseased one (2 Cor 6:16). Concern for health is a wholesome witness to a God who created us whole. The body is to glorify God (1 Cor 6:16-20) and be glorified by God (1 Cor 15:51-57). Every fleshly temple will be whole then. Heaven will be free from all disease and suffering. Perhaps the healing miracles of Christ are his way of bearing witness to the final glory we will receive.

Some day in that new world his church will sit down in the councils of heaven. Those who died of plague, leukemia, polio and the "thousand natural shocks that flesh is heir to" will be there. Then they will not remember the awful pain that closed their window of existence. Nor will they remember the long-ago world of bacteria, infection and death. Millions of believers will glorify God in bodies that will never experience a headache or a bruise. The only scars left in the entire universe will be the stigmata of Christ which the Father will leave in his hands so that we will remember how much he loves us.

Spiritual warfare is just as brutal as human warfare.
Rimbaud

Imps and eager caucus
Raffle for our souls—
Emily Dickinson

I, Lucifer, Satan, Demon
Once visible, despised, shunned by earthlings.
Learning from men to disguise
Go underground
Now incognito—
Courted, templed, Madison-avenued;
Educated, elevated, sophisticated
Retooling men's minds.
Musetta Gilman

10
The
Other
Kingdom

EXORCISMS ARE MIRACLES of supernatural conflict. They represent Christ's most strategic miracles because they are God's direct invasion of the Satanic world. Still they seem to be the miracles doubted the most. They assume the reality of both Satan and his demons. How lightly we regard Satan's kingdom can be seen in the fact that we call football teams the Blue Devils or a car the Demon.

Nowadays demons smack a little too much of Halloween to merit serious discussion. Aren't devils and ghosts and "things that go bump in the night" a little like fingernails scraping down a blackboard—weird but explainable in ordinary terms?

In Jesus' day, Satan and his kingdom were viewed seriously. Satan was wisely feared. The people of the Gerasenes tried to bind Legion in chains and keep him under guard. Jesus' courage stands in contrast to their fear. But he still took the situation as seriously as the rest (Lk 8:26-39). More important, Jesus' spiritual perception was so honed that he quickly saw every authentic Satanic invasion of his Father's world. The enemy might try to camouflage himself in the clever disguise of an epileptic. Jesus saw him clearly even when his less perceptive disciples believed the deception (Mt 17:14-21).

Satan and Adam

Satan's work is real. It caused Adam to cower in the shadows with half-eaten fruit. Until his disobedience, he had known only the external snake—the python in the tree. But having tasted the fruit, he came to know the serpent as a writhing, ghastly, inner blackness.

But Adam was not possessed in the same way the Gerasene demoniac was. His will had not lost its identity in Satan. Adam wept as he left Eden. He knew that Satan, who had destroyed his relationship with God, could ultimately destroy his life. A leper does not cry because he has lost a finger but because he knows that the same insidious principle will claim his arm. Satan's goal was more than fouling Eden. It was subjugating all of humanity.

Adam and Satan had both been disobedient: Satan with his angelic insurrection and Adam with his gluttonous caprice. They had both hurt their majestic Creator. They were both in exile: Adam from Eden, Satan from Paradise. Both were incapable of being totally good any longer.

Satan was more powerful than Adam. But Adam had something that Satan wanted. Satan had been thrown out of heaven, and he was not one to take his exile lightly. In Adam, man became a battlefield for the war of good and evil.

Adam knew he would be a partisan battlefield and would take God's side in the conflict. But the new, inner darkness left him unable to live up to his good intentions. Adam, however, had a great-grandson many centuries later. When his mother, Mary, lifted Jesus from the straw, she sensed the struggle that would belong to him, but she knew he would win.

In the wilderness at the beginning of his ministry, Jesus vowed that the mistake of Adam would not be repeated. Satan's desire for Jesus was no different than it had been for Adam. Like Adam, Jesus was offered the apple of world power, instant fame and knowledge. But Jesus did not yield as Adam did. He gloried in obedience to God. Christ confronted Satan in strength. So Jesus held fast to his sinlessness through Gethsemane, blessing his crucifiers. Triumphantly Christ stood against Satan till at last he won over death.

Jesus was victorious, but the rest of mankind since Eden has lost the struggle with evil. Some offered the deceiver so much that he grasped their whole being. Once inside, Satan's invisible angels made the hapless marionettes work. Their victims shrieked and danced at the end of all hope. They bellowed obscenities, flexed their tendons, broke chains and gnawed the bars. The unholy light of hell burned in their yellow eyes. Wisely, most feared the demonic, for they knew that they could become what they beheld.

This universal fear causes me to view the exorcisms as being among the chief of Jesus' miracles. A healed pancreas merely provides a normal insulin supply, but an exorcism involves a direct confrontation with ancient spiritual warriors. These glimpses of eternal warfare are the previews of the final subjugation of Satan.

For all their reality demons are usually left in the first century. Occasionally playwrights and novelists tempt us to believe they still exist. But for most they are only fictional horror. I do not believe this is at all the case. In my own ministry two or three times I have confronted persons I believe were under an alien, supernatural control. I have known other pastors who had similar encounters. While I don't want to recount these experiences in detail, they are nonetheless very real.

Restless Spirits

Demons are spiritual beings hostile to God and to humans who serve as the agents of Satan. While demons are not so prominent in Old Testament literature, Isaiah (13:21) referred to the desolation of Israel with the somber warning that their empty houses (perhaps haunted houses) would "be full of howling creatures" and satyrs, the goat-gods which later became the symbols of Satanic worship.

Demons are always looking for a house or home to reside in. In their search for a place to live, they are more fond of earth than either hell or outer space. In the beleaguered demoniac, they beg Jesus to send them into the pigs rather than back to the abyss (Lk 8:32). Interestingly, Jesus permits this. It is not, however, because of an antipork, Jewish bias. Rather, the unwelcome demons enter the pigs, so the demoniac has visible assurance that the demons are really gone.

Satan, like his underlings, is also a restless seeker. Job 1:7 says he has been "going to and fro on the earth." And Peter calls this same wandering personality "your adversary" who "prowls around like a roaring lion, seeking some one to devour" (1 Pet 5:8).

Why this restlessness? Both Isaiah 14 and Revelation 12 describe the struggle in heaven in which Satan loses his station. There is no place for him in the presence of God. The heavens are boarded up, and the earth will soon be closed to his presence. He is lashing about the world for he knows that the time of his exile is short (Rev 12:12). The demons, those angels who joined him in his insurrection (Rev 12:7-9), join him in his homelessness.

When Satan's coup failed, they spread across the earth, cheering and encouraging evil. Every ghastly happenstance of history bears grim evidence of their existence. The ovens at Auschwitz, the Stalinist reforms, mass murders in Texas and

Cambodian "relocation" are the testimonies to the reality of demonic evil. Of course, we should be careful about multiplying demons so much that we are no longer responsible for our own sins and errors. Living in a world of too many demons is as unrealistic as not believing in them at all. Sincere clerics and earnest laymen frequently try to exorcise the "demon of despondency" or the "demon of laziness" or the "demon of five-card stud." Suddenly we have no sins to confess because "the devil made me do it."

Whatever demons are, however, we must pledge ourselves not to give them too much importance by paying too much attention to them. Theologians of the Middle Ages also overdid their descriptions of the Satanic realm. Much of it was not drawn from the Bible. Thus we need to sift carefully the Satanic lore that we encounter.

Some Christians in our own time often give Satan more credit than he deserves. One gets the impression that they have split the universe exactly in two: into Satan and Christ, well-matched generalissimos, poised, ready to fight it out at Armageddon.

The demons we pursue may not seem as exciting as those we see in the movies and novels of our day. William Blake, the English engraver, in a moment of poetic rapture claimed that he had actually seen the funeral of a woodland fairy. W. B. Yeats, the Irish poet, stated that this proved the inferiority of English fairies as the Irish fairies were immortal! When we begin speculating on the nature of demons, we are in danger of making them altogether unbelievable.

The Pharisees seemed to think that Jesus was paranoid, always looking over his shoulder for an assassin. So they accused him of having a demon (Jn 7:20). When they said he was able to cast out demons because he himself was demon possessed, it was a colloquial slur (Mt 12:24). Today one would say, "The man is insane to make such a statement!"

Exorcisms are often viewed with skepticism in our country, but not in places where demons are an accepted part of a primitive culture. I have two missionary friends who have worked in animistic cultures. Both of them have shared with me chilling stories of demonic encounters. While I have never had such a direct encounter, I am, through their experiences, more convinced of the existence of supernatural foes.

The Demon of Direct Attack

In Jesus' ministry, only six exorcisms are described in detail. Every one was a skirmish in a spiritual war that has been going on throughout time. And while demons are not categorized in the New Testament, let me look at these exorcisms to illustrate five different types.

The first demon is the sacrilege demon. Christian demonology does not assign a name to this evil spirit, but the Hindus call him the Asura demon. He dares to confront the omnipotence of God. In a sense, his behavior is described in classic form in the book of Job as Satan arrogantly struts into the court of heaven. In 2 Baruch 29:4 this spirit of antitruth is pictured as the spirit of the great Leviathan, the evil monster of chaos. He is the spirit of evil that reared its head against God (Is 14:12-21). He goes brazenly to church and disrupts worship with slanderous irreverence. In Mark 1:21-28 this demon disrupted the synagogue by wailing in terror.

William Peter Blatty's novel *The Exorcist* describes the Asura demon. Obscenities to the Lord and confrontation and challenge to God are his methods. He seems to be a kamikaze, knowing that his direct challenge to God is suicidal. Nonetheless, he goes through with it. He is the prototype of all other demons, brilliant in venom and sacrilege.

I was once fortunate enough to know a great missionary

who had worked in primitive sections of Africa in the 1920s and 1930s. Henry was a superb linguist who went in to bush villages and reduced dialects to alphabets so he could teach the natives to read. He began his ministry in each village by building a small straw hut for his work. These little schools were walled in bamboo and thatched with straw. They were also the center of attack by the resident shaman who saw education as the enemy of religion in the tribe.

On one occasion, Henry was warned by a witch doctor that if he did not leave the village, the tribal god would burn the school to the ground. While Henry had no fear of tribal gods, he did keep his eye on the witch doctor, who he thought might try to set his school ablaze. But to his utter amazement Henry felt the grip of fear when in the wee hours of the morning, a great clap of thunder and a jagged bolt of lightning destroyed the school.

The next morning the witch doctor came early with his tribal retinue to ask my friend to leave. But this man of God replied that the voodoo god would not have the last word. That night, Henry said, the great God of the Bible would strike the shaman's totem with lightning. The people of the village were as excited by this proposition as the Baal worshipers had been on Mt. Carmel.

Henry was stunned at his own words. What had he done? What was the impulse? The gauntlet, once cast, could not be retracted. But he could pray. And pray, he did. In the early morning hours the tribal totem was also struck by a bolt of lightning. It too burned to the ground. The missionary stayed. The school was rebuilt. The alphabet came, along with enlightenment.

Destroyer and Death

The next type of demon, the antimatter demon, also has no

name among Christians. But the Hindus call him the Rakshasa demon. It is the Rakshasa that corresponds to Satan in the Revelation of St. John. His name in the Apocalypse is Apollyon or Abaddon, the Destroyer (Rev 9:11).

The name Destroyer indicates Satan's feeling about matter. Remember all matter exists because of the creation of God. If you wish to hurt a creative person, you cannot do it more effectively than to smash what he or she has made. If you are angry with a porcelain artist and want to strike him with vengeance, just enter his studio and pull his figurines from their shelves.

Some years ago in the Vatican I stood before Michelangelo's great Pietà. I thought of the artist working alone, absorbed in his creation, hitting the chisel in tender sanctity. Somberness and shame came over me. The artist's labor liberated the mother of our Lord in her awful bereavement from her stony captivity. Since 1499 she has sat there in sorrow holding her executed son. The artist had cut from stone the deepest reverence of his soul.

But some years ago, an assailant came. An Apollyon leapt the barrier with his hammer and defaced the great masterpiece. This is how Satan, the spirit of Rakshasa, feels about the work of God. Smash it; mar it; deface it; write graffiti on the finished work of the universe!

There are two exorcisms of the mute demoniacs (Mt 9:32-34; 12:22). Satan resented the creation of speech as he did all of God's works. Then came the Rakshasa! He smashes the motor coordination, shuts up the larynx and curses the tongue. And the work of God is smashed. Man, created to speak, is mute. But Christ comes! The demon is exorcised.

A third category of demons, defined by the church during the Middle Ages, was called the Boggart or the graveyard demon. A derivative of the word *Boggart* has survived in the word *boogieman*. Originally Boggarts were the psychopathic

demons. Legion turned the man of the Gerasenes into an un-
manageable monster who broke chains (Lk 8:29). So he lived
among the tombs as the village madman. Perhaps some said
that when the moon was full, his powers were immense, and
no earthly chain could hold him. "He even robs the graves and
feasts as a ghoul," they might have insisted. On murky nights
one could hear him crying aloud in the graveyard.

But his curse was loneliness. Ripped from society and stuck
in a tombyard, immense storms of evil ripped his heart. He
wanted love but the alien beings that crowded his life would
not permit him the luxury of friends. They devoured his mind.

Graveyards are a testament to the separation of life and
death. The Boggart reminds us that hell, ultimate separation,
is the final state of those who refuse Christ on earth. Though
we are communal beings, we are shut up in the walls of torment, isolated by pain. Those dying outside of Christ often
find solace in saying they will not be the only ones in hell. But
when we are separated from life, we find no crowds. Torment
closes us in to ourselves. Friends do not exist.

The Gerasene demoniac had a foretaste of hell. Satan had
cut him off from the world. But Jesus cast out the separating
demon. At last he was no longer a feared night monster. He
could enter the world of shops and parks. Christ had given him
the gift of oneness with his world. He had discovered the greatest secret of the Christian faith, abiding togetherness. "Lo, I
am with you always" (Mt 28:20).

The Incubus is the fourth kind of demon. Superstitious
church leaders of the Middle Ages classified this as the demon
of sexual distortion. We find no clear evidence of this demon
in Jesus' teaching. But medieval commentators said the inner
nature of the Incubus was characterized by the same lust that
lured the fallen angels from the rim of glory to seduce the earth
women in Genesis 6:1-2. Although Jesus taught that angels

were not permitted marriage (Mt 22:30), in I Corinthians 11:10 Paul may be suggesting that angels have some sexuality.

Whether or not the Incubus has any validity as a sexual being, we may be confident that sexuality, as a creation of God, is a target for Apollyon. Throughout Christianity, illicit sex has been the slur of witches' covens on the dignity of true faith. In our day, Satan has already defaced biblical sexuality to the point that it has little respect in our suave, modern culture.

The fifth and final demon is the Imp or the demon of mischief. The boy of Matthew 17:14, described as an epileptic, suffered under the trickery of an inner foe. Sometimes the child fell into the water or fire. Always it looked like an accident, but always it was the result of the demon who threw him into such circumstances. This is characteristic of demonic Imps.

The destructive tendencies of the Imp closely resemble those of the Rakshasa, the antimatter demon. This should not surprise us since the continuing goal of Apollyon Satan is to destroy all that God made.

The Enemy of God and Satan

These categories are, of course, too rigid. Demons are hard to identify. In Matthew 17, the disciples had some trouble curing the boy because they do not know whether they were really pursuing epilepsy or an Imp. Luke 8:2 says Mary Magdalene once had seven devils, though some theologians suggest that Jesus' use of the term *seven devils* is symbolic, identifying Mary as an adulteress who violated the seventh commandment. But my hope is that this discussion will help us better understand how demons affect those which they inhabit.

Healthy faith retains a belief in the demonic realm. Satan stands opposite God, but he is not an equal or an opposite dark force in the universe. Satan's power only appears great when he brings it against the weakness of human will.

Skepticism is the enemy of both God and Satan. No one does God service who disbelieves in Satan. And those who disbelieve in personified evil soon cease to believe in personified good as well. Here is the weakness of some contemporary theology. When Satan is dismissed, God becomes elusive.

Exorcisms foreshadow the final victory of God over Satan. Ultimately the universe will be swept clean of evil's horrible reality. God will take the key to the great pit and call Leviathan into it forever. God and Adam will walk together once more in the cool of the day. The tree of the knowledge of good and evil will have its roots exposed, and the new Eden will never know the slithering of serpents.

Most of the world is either asleep or dead. The religious people are, for the most part, asleep. The irreligious are dead.
Thomas Merton

Humankind cannot bear very much reality.
T. S. Eliot

*The ancient man approached God (or even the gods)
as the accused person approaches his judge. For the modern
man the roles are reversed. He is the judge:
God is in the dock. He is quite a kindly judge: If God
should have a reasonable defense for being the god who permits
war, poverty and disease, he is ready to listen to it.*
C. S. Lewis

II
Of
Mystery
and
Madness

CHRISTIANITY IS THE bread of life to those of us who believe and a quaint affliction to those who don't. Our love of mystery makes us look like madmen. After all, we feed on such strange teachings as the Trinity and the resurrection. We hold to Christ's unexplained yet powerful life which we feel stirring inside our own. The sane, those who having examined Christianity clinically, have decided that faith is somehow beneath their rational dignity.

We who believe should accept the profile of madness but make it clear that our madness is not the same kind of mental splintering that Nietzsche (one of the sane) endured the last eleven years of his life. Nor is it the same disorientation that the Marquis de Sade (another of the sane) experienced at the Charenton Lunatick Asylum. Millions of us have been liberated by this mystery, not enslaved.

Our "illogical" faith is a happy madness. And as Polonius said of the "demented" Prince Hamlet, "Though this be madness, yet there is method in it."

Christian madness was born in the mystery of New Testament faith. Jesus faced many of the same charges against his sanity that his followers also faced. The sane of the first century said to him, "You are mad!" So how shall we ever hope to escape such slurs? Christ himself said, "A servant is not greater than his master; nor is he who is sent greater than he who sent him" (Jn 13:16). Jesus also reminded his followers, "Woe to you, when all men speak well of you" (Lk 6:26). Perhaps this can be used as a reliable guide to the seriousness of our devotion. When we cross the threshold of faith, our reputation may become controversial. Some will admire our conversion, but many will feel that our convictions are extreme, our habits "churchy" and our devotion overdone.

The Get-Ready Man

James Thurber told of a thin and lanky prophet who went around Thurber's boyhood hometown crying, "Get ready! Get ready! The world is coming to an end!" The community called him the Get-Ready Man. Whatever his appearance might have been, the Get-Ready Man was right: the world is coming to an end. Probably the Get-Ready Man went about it wrong, but the story reflects the tongue-in-cheek attitude which the sane of our generation have toward the committed. To these, all Christians have a madness only moderately different from that of the Get-Ready Man.

I wonder how Thurber would have reacted to John the Baptist. If ever there was a Get-Ready Man, John was it. He was unkempt, dressed only in camel's hair and a leather girdle. He looked as though he had just swung in from the jungle. He shouted with embarrassing volume, "Get ready; the kingdom of God is at hand." Doubtless, some thought John overpreached. Certainly the queen thought so. She did not like him meddling in her sophisticated sexual intrigues. But Jesus said of God's Get-Ready Man, "Among those born of women there has risen no one greater than John the Baptist" (Mt 11:11).

In the space age real faith often appears insane because God himself seems out of date. Most moderns have a hard time conceiving of God as contemporary. He is rather a white-haired, flowing-robed fresco imprisoned on the ceiling of the Sistine Chapel. This archaic God is out of tune with the time and enshrouded in images of yesterday.

Neither books nor movies have helped to establish our sanity. Throughout the media we are stereotyped. In snide fiction Christians are mocked or challenged beyond their ability to defend themselves. The faith iteslf is often attacked by subthemes of hypocrisy. Such slurs make Christianity's great heart of mystery appear all the more illogical.

My point is to emphasize the difficulty of serving God's reputation and ours at the same time. If we are to follow Christ, our security must depend on something besides having all "men speak well" of us.

Not all charges of madness, however, are direct. On the day of Pentecost, Peter and his friends were filled with the ecstasy of the Spirit of God. Being more amused than frightened, the sane jostled each other, elbow to rib cage, and said, "This is an amusing kind of epilepsy. These Christians are full of new wine!" Everybody in Acts 2 seemed to be having a good time. The Christians were giddy with the Spirit and the sane with the sideshow. Perhaps even Peter was laughing when he got up and said, "I know what you're thinking, but it isn't wine. Not even Christians get drunk at nine in the morning." Their joyful madness, however, did rather resemble that utter bliss that fades into a hangover rather than any serious affliction of mind.

The Holy Spirit then clothed the church with power and charged her with life. His mysterious action led the faithful to follow with what seemed like a radical madness.

Paul, the Apostle of Madness

Things were different back in those days when Christians still drank a little. Now many are prohibitionist teetotalers, and their madness is seldom confused with drunkenness. The sane can better understand believers who drink than zealots whose doctrine has gone wild.

St. Paul is often blamed, mistakenly, for the unfortunate state of this mad mystique of Christians. The thinking runs like this: In contrast to Peter the evangelist, Paul was a theologian. Evangelists can see the humor in everything and sometimes load their revivalism with jokes and happy hymns. This kind of madness at least seems a happy affliction. Theologians, on the other hand, appear to have a worse kind of lunacy. They meditate in gray cells and agonize over every "neo-anything" that seems to threaten the faith. They rave about the church's great teachings and work furiously to harmonize them with logic and sanity.

St. Paul, however, was no such theologian. Rather he demonstrated best what it meant to be a madman. Paul once stood before King Agrippa to help the King understand the great mystery of the resurrection. Festus, a Roman who also listened to Paul's explanation, said at its conclusion, "Paul, you are mad; your great learning is turning you mad." Paul protested, "I am not, most excellent Festus, but I am speaking the sober truth" (Acts 26:23-25). But alas, to the Romans Paul's explanation was unconvincing and Festus went unconverted.

Paul had earlier experienced the same kinds of accusations on Mars Hill when the Athenians made fun of his obsession with the resurrection (Acts 17:18, 32). Thus Paul learned to cope with the image of madness he projected. There are several indications from his writings that group opinion had chipped

Paul's confidence in his sound mentality, and he pleaded, "Let no one think me foolish; but even if you do, accept me as a fool" (2 Cor 11:16). Or again he said, "I am speaking as a fool. . . . I am talking like a madman" (2 Cor 11:21, 23).

Earlier he wrote that the "word of the cross is folly to those who are perishing" (1 Cor 1:18). Indeed, he said, "It pleased God through the folly of what we preach to save those who believe" (1 Cor 1:21). Not only was Paul aware that his convictions made him look like a fool, but he also knew that for the sane of his day the entire Christian faith looked like a bulky slice of insanity in contrast to the orderly and popular Olympic religions.

Unnecessary Madness

Paul had one other significant word on Christian madness: some Christians, Paul felt, were needlessly fostering the impression that Christians were mad by a showy and incoherent worship service in which they got carried away with their emotions and spoke in an "unknown tongue." Paul reminded the Corinthians that you can make more converts with a spoonful of order than you can with a barrelful of *glossolalia*. He put it to them rather bluntly: "If, therefore, the whole church assembles and all speak in tongues, and outsiders or unbelievers enter, will they not say that you are mad?" (2 Cor 14:23).

Christian tradition is filled with those who followed the Corinthian example. St. Simon, the pillar saint, withdrew to the top of a pillar to live away from the tainted and the secular world. In our day he would have been the target of Halloween pranksters with air rifles. Most who saw him sitting up there month after month, rain or shine, would do everything they could to avoid Christianity. Anyone who became a Christian would apparently have to become a dimwitted aerialist too.

Other early Christians often appeared less intelligent than

they might have if they had managed to put into practice the saying that cleanliness is next to godliness. Since they considered nudity a sin, they also considered bathing a sin. As strange as it sounds, the stronger their upwind aroma, the more devout they were regarded to be.

St. Jerome wrote to St. Paula encouraging her not to tempt Satan by taking a bath. The advice may have been superfluous since most of the virgins were so unkempt as to tempt no one, Satan notwithstanding. One of these early saints was cited for his supreme holiness by the fact that lice dripped from his body as he walked to worship. The sheer filth in which the faith of that day was incubated must have kept many away from the nonantiseptic madness called Christianity.

Bertrand Russell spoke of one particular order of nuns who, for decades always wore their robes while bathing. Their reason: "The great God can see through bathroom walls." So to always appear decent before him, they took baths fully robed. Never did they seem to understand that a God whose miraculous vision could pierce walls could also pierce robes.

Fortunately, Christians are no longer unsanitary in their madness. There are no pillar saints like Simon. But there are plenty of modern madnesses in the church. Anything from high-powered, Bible-thumping, finger-pointing evangelists to unquestioning devotion to intricate gothic dogma may frighten the most open-minded. Some kinds of madness are, however, more respectable than others. An insanity that loves Christ with a Latin Mass is generally seen as more elite than a madness which enjoys a gospel quartet. If you want a degree of respectability to go along with your Christianity, it might be best to become an Episcopalian. But fundamentalist churches can only be recommended for those who want to go fully and immediately berserk.

The denomination I belong to offers a moderate madness.

As a middle-of-the-road church, its coefficient of insanity is just about halfway between the Pentecostals and the Episcopalians. If you suddenly rose in a service and gave an unsolicited Quaker testimony, your madness would be unacceptable. Likewise, footwashing would never be allowed, even if you supplied your own basin. On the other hand, your madness would be just as great if you wanted to discuss Thomas Merton or apostolic succession seriously. Genuflecting at the communion table would indicate total insanity.

I know I can never make my own moderate madness acceptable to the sane. Still, like most in my church, I feel secure between Billy Sunday and the Archbishop of Canterbury—mad enough to believe in mystery but not so mad as to scare away skeptics.

The sane, you see, have a twofold problem in seeking to evaluate the mad. Simply put, they are suspicious and they are confused. Their suspicions come largely because they live outside the church. They do not understand her sacraments or ordinances. They feed on hearsay:

"Catholics believe Mary saves."

"Presbyterians believe 'dancin' is a sin.' "

"Lutherans are anti-Mason."

"Baptists think that they are the only ones going to heaven."

"Methodists won't drink in front of each other."

Knowing only enough to be suspicious of all but not enough to come to faith in any, they live in confusion and doubt. The early church had the same problem. The Romans didn't understand its mysterious nature. Churches had no buildings. They always met in homes or rented halls or parks or catacombs. The Romans heard that the Christians always talked about love and nearly always met at night. They assumed, therefore, that they met for immoral purposes. Further, they heard that these Christians always talked about the body and blood of

Christ. Presumably this meant they secretly practiced cannibalism.

When Rome burned, it was naturally blamed on this new sect of illegal and insane Christians. They began to die for Roman sport, and for two hundred fifty years they were the whipping post of the emperors' frustrations. They died because of their adherence to a madness that the Romans could not understand.

Let Us Have Madness

We know that our faith, though mysterious, brings joy. We can endure the charges of being crazy because of the light that has come upon us. Meaning and destiny mean more to us than a sane reputation.

We are somehow like the man possessed by the legion. He was mad and untamed, fierce in his condition. He was convulsed by fevered spasms, and lights that no one saw but dove at him in searing brilliance. Probably when his seizures were over, he collapsed in sobbing. He was fierce and to be feared. And because he was feared, he was friendless.

Then he met Jesus, the Christ. It is a dramatic lesson in redeeming peace. Suddenly the madman is smiling into Christ's compassion. His soul is swept clean by gentle eyes and a clear mind. Christ's hands, yet unscarred, touch him and the universe is instantly ordered. The strange world of "things" is no longer surging or threatening. The lights which screamed are gone.

At last the man is clothed. He sits by the disciples' campfire probing his wonderful world of order. He smiles at Jesus with childish adoration and laughs a free man's laugh. He is a slate waiting to be chalked with the message of love. Jesus has covered all his senseless surgings with peace.

Did the story stop there? What happened to the man when

he met his first skeptic? At what point in his radiant relationship with Christ did he begin to realize that some thought a new madness had replaced the old? Someone inevitably told him that he had traded his diving lights for a fanatic infatuation. A scholar of his day was sure to tell him that his whole experience of grace was to be pitied. A well-meaning apothecary might have suggested a little posttrauma therapy. However it happened, sooner or later the man discovered that the sane did not believe his tale of redemption.

But however they assessed his Christ-affliction, he didn't mind. He had known both kinds of insanity, and he was in love with his new affliction. Like him, we who now believe find great meaning in our madness. It is because of that meaning that we even dare to tell others about it. It is not presumption that makes us feel like we have something to offer the sane. We have seen the sane and felt honest compassion for their joyless sanity. We grant them their right to reject Christ, and yet we are touched by their malnourishment. Like lepers at a feast, we invite them to share our mystery even if they believe we are cankered with madness. Ah, we love our madness for in it is life. Thus we cry to our world the very words of Kenneth Paatchen, "Let us have madness openly, Oh, men of my generation."

Notes

Chapter 3: Against Absurdity

[1]William March, *Unknown Soldier*.

[2]Michael Green, *Runaway World* (Downers Grove, Ill.: InterVarsity Press, 1968), p. 39.

[3]Bertolt Brecht, *Galileo* (New York: Grove Press, 1966), p. 81.

[4]Victor Frankl, *Man's Search for Meaning* (New York: Washington Square Press, 1963), p. 160.

[5]Henry Miller, *The Tropic of Cancer,* as quoted in Hans Rookmaaker, *Modern Art and the Death of a Culture* (Downers Grove, Ill.: InterVarsity Press, 1970), p. 146.

[6]Kurt Schwitters, *Ursonate* (Hanover: Merzverlag) quoted in Rookmaaker, p. 145.

[7]Johann Neuhauster, *What Was It Like in the Concentration Camp at Dachau?* (Munich: Manz, 1973), pp. 76-77.

Chapter 4: What Matter?

[1]Adam Smith, *The Money Game* (New York: Dell, 1969), p. 80.

[2]Elton Trueblood, *The Company of the Committed* (New York: Harper & Row, 1961), p. 15.

Chapter 5: The Student of Christ

[1]William Shakespeare, *King Henry VIII*, Act III, Scene ii.

[2]Karl Jaspers, *The Future of Mankind*, as quoted in Martin E. Marty, *Varieties of Unbelief* (Garden City, N.Y.: Doubleday, 1966), p. 211.

[3]Leo Tolstoy, *Memoirs of a Lunatic* from *The Existential Imagination*, edited by Frederick Karl and Leo Hamilton (New York: Fawcett Pub., 1963), pp. 75-76.

Chapter 7: Meaning in Miracles

[1]André Malraux, *The Walnut Trees of Altenbert*, as quoted in Maurka Friedman, *To Deny Our Nothingness* (London: Gollancz, 1967), p. 17, quoted by Colin Chapman, *Christianity on Trial* (Wheaton, Ill.: Tyndale, 1975), p. 174.

[2]G. K. Chesterton, *Orthodoxy* (Garden City, N.Y.: Doubleday, 1959), p. 127.

Chapter 8: The Miracle of Life

[1]Paul Little, *Know Why You Believe* (Downers Grove, Ill.: InterVarsity Press, 1968), p. 25.